FOOD ADDICTION

Your Brain is Stronger than your Belly.

Binge No More, How to Stop Compulsive Eating

Judith Martin

© Copyright 2023 by Judith Martin - All rights reserved.

This document is geared towards providing exact and reliable information in regard to the topic and issue covered.

- From a Declaration of Principles which was accepted and approved equally by a Committee of the American Bar Association and a Committee of Publishers and Associations.

In no way is it legal to reproduce, duplicate, or transmit any part of this document in either electronic means or in printed format. All rights reserved.

The information provided herein is stated to be truthful and consistent, in that any liability, in terms of inattention or otherwise, by any usage or abuse of any policies, processes, or directions contained within is the solitary and utter responsibility of the recipient reader. Under no circumstances will any legal responsibility or blame be held against the publisher for any reparation, damages, or monetary loss due to the information herein, either directly or indirectly.

Respective authors own all copyrights not held by the publisher.

The information herein is offered for informational purposes solely and is universal as so. The presentation of the information is without contract or any type of guarantee assurance.

The trademarks that are used are without any consent, and the publication of the trademark is without permission or backing by the trademark owner. All trademarks and brands within this book are for clarifying purposes only and are owned by the owners themselves, not affiliated with this document.

Table of Contents

Introduction 5

Chapter 1. Binge Eating Problem: Who Binges?. 7

Chapter 2. Psychological And Social Aspects Of Binge Eating Disorder... 12

    What Causes Eating Problems? 14

    Binge Eating and Addiction 33

    The Treatment of Binge Eating Disorder............. 34

    Diets-Calorie Restriction, Low-Fat Diets, Low-Carb, Diets - DON'T Work 38

    Ignoring our hunger Signals Results in Food Obsession and Often Binge Eating Later 47

    Focusing On Weight Instead Of Health and Nutrition Is Not Helpful and Actually Can Lead Us to Unhealthy Behavior 48

Chapter 3. Manage Hunger In 9 Moves............ 52

Chapter 4. The Mindfulness-Based Eating Solutions 69

Chapter 5. What Are You Really, Really Hungry For? 87

Chapter 6. Making "Healthy Fast Food" In A Hurry-Up World 107

    The Perils of Convenience Eating 107

    Junk Food. Because We Like It and How to Do Without

It 110

An Extra Benefit of Cooking At Home 114

Healthy Fast Food Defined 116

Organic, Local, or Seasonal Ingredients........... 118

Continuing On the Path of Mindful Eating and Living 120

Your Personal Plan of Action........................... 120

Mindfulness Meditation Practice 121

Conclusion.. 123

Introduction

Several pieces of research say that binge eating disorder is one of the most frequent types of eating disorders that can be found in the USA. Binge stands for eating large amounts of food in a short amount of time. The biggest difference between binge eating disorder and other eating disorders is that people with BED don't throw up their food. Binge eating can lead to serious health problems, but with proper treatment, it can be dealt with.

Two key features can be used to describe binge eating disorder. The first feature is the fact that people who have BED will eat large portions of food in very short amounts of time (let's say to eat at least double than the average person in just an hour or two). The second feature of binge eating disorder that you can recognize is that a person has a control loss while eating. People who are not able to stop themselves from eating are actually binging. We will discuss reasons for developing binge eating disorder, but it is important to remember that they can be different and that they are usually a combination of several factors (it can be a product of genetic predispositions or cultural and social factors, and so on.).

Those who binge can be of different genders and ages too. This eating disorder appears regardless of someone's cultural background or socio-economic position. When it comes to gender vulnerability to this eating disorder, one can argue that there is an equal number of men and women having a binge eating disorder. Some studies suggest that there are more females having BED issues, but there are others who claim that there is approximately the same number of both genders having issues with binging.

Chapter 1

Binge Eating Problem: Who Binges?

A difference between the person who suffers from binge eating disorder and the person who has issues with other eating disorders is that there is no self-induced vomiting. The person who binges doesn't show signs of so-called "compensatory behavior", which means that they don't go exercising too much after they eat nor do they decide to vomit immediately after the meal to avoid gaining weight. Therefore, it is not surprising that most of those who binge also have issues with obesity or are overweight.

So, who binges?

Those who eat frequently without any control. As we already explained, those who suffer from binge eating disorder eat enormous amounts of food and without proper breaks between meals. When having a binge-eating episode, a person is unable to stop eating even if they want to do so. Their need for uncontrolled eating is stronger than their will to stop at that moment.

Those who binge have certain eating habits that can be identified. The simplest ones are quick eating or eating large amounts of food without being actually (physically) hungry. This also includes the necessity to eat even if they start feeling uncomfortable because they have already passed the point of being full.

People who binge often feel shame and guilt. These emotions are typical of those with binge eating problems. These feelings are frequently caused by the amount and way of eating they have during their binge episodes that we already mentioned above. Binging is used to confront challenging emotional states, and it is usually caused by stress or boredom and anger.

Binging also means that a person will have certain behavior around food. As we just explained, those who suffer from binge eating disorder use it to deal with different emotions, and because of that, they can develop eating habits that are a bit different. For example, many of those who have BED prefer eating alone, and they don't feel comfortable with having others around while they are eating.

However, this doesn't mean that everyone who eats too much or doesn't like to eat in front of others suffers from binge eating disorder. There are certain criteria that one must meet to be diagnosed with this eating disorder. Some of the clearest symptoms are:

There has to be a certain period in which a person eats excessive amounts of food. These periods in which one eats large portions of food are known as binge episodes (we mentioned them as one of the key characteristics of those who binge). This criterion includes loss of control over their eating and the fact that they can't stop the episode.

Now, eating a lot in a short amount of time can happen even without having BED. That is why we would like to point out a few more characteristics that a person should have to be diagnosed with binge eating problem:

- The binge episode eating will normally be much faster than normal eating.
- A person can even feel uncomfortable because he or she has already eaten too much, but that doesn't stop them.
- There is no physical hunger when the person starts having a binge episode
- Binge eaters suffer embarrassment about the way they eat and the amount eaten during a binge episode, which is why people with BED prefer to eat alone.
- They experience feelings of guilt, disgust, and depression. People who suffer from binge eating disorder often have a bad attitude about themselves after their binge episodes.

There is a certain pattern that has to be followed to be sure that a person is potentially suffering from BED. It is usual that they have a binge episode at least once each week for a period in excess of three months. Otherwise, it can be seen as stress eating without health consequences that can be too serious.

Another serious eating disorder that has spread

through the world is called bulimia nervosa. However, there is one major difference between bulimia nervosa and BED. Unlike the first disorder, the binge-eating problem doesn't involve extreme behaviors that are related to weight loss. As we mentioned, professionally, these behaviors are known as "compensatory", and they are often extreme and can end up having permanent and serious consequences. Still, if a person suffers from a disorder known as anorexia nervosa, it is not uncommon for the following symptoms, which include binge eating ones. And while it is true that anorexia nervosa involves extreme dieting it doesn't mean that it automatically excludes binge-eating problems as a diagnosis either.

The most recent statistics say that approximately 3.5% of females have binge eating problems in the USA. When it comes to men and adolescents, about 2% of men and 1.6% of adolescents have issues with this eating disorder. BED can be developed regardless of the ethnicity or race of the person. Still, we can point out a few groups that can be more vulnerable to binge eating disorder than others.

Firstly, people who are dieting frequently have bigger chances of ending up binge eating. Some researchers say that the chances are even 12 times bigger than for those who don't use any dieting programs. Also, it is scientifically proven that BED has a bigger impact on younger people rather than on older people. The average age for developing BED is between the early and mid-twenties. However, that doesn't mean that older people (especially women) don't have binge eating problems.

Two out of three people dealing with binge eating issues are obese. Nevertheless, being overweight is not the only health risk that comes from BED. Obesity, in general, can be a cause for many health problems like increased levels of cholesterol or high blood pressure. Furthermore, there are several types of cancer that obese people can suffer from such cancers as kidney cancer, pancreatic cancer, breast cancer, uterine cancer, thyroid cancer, and so forth. For females, obesity can cause problems with the menstrual cycle. Long-term, this means that being overweight can prevent their ovulation, which can make it hard for women to have children.

Chapter 2

Psychological And Social Aspects Of Binge Eating Disorder

Binge eating disorder can affect both the mind and the body in multiple aspects. Some signs, such as physical, psychological and behavioral can help with diagnosing BED. The most common signs of people who are dealing with binge eating problems are sleeping issues, the fact that they are tired all the time, developing intolerance to certain food types and focusing on food and their body shape. Also, these people often feel extremely dissatisfied with their looks, which further leads to anxiety, sadness, and guilt.

People who have binge eating disorder often have low self-esteem and they are extremely sensitive when someone comments on their body or their food choices. The feeling of anxiety can lead to irritability and other behavioral signs (hiding food around the house, evading weight and food questions). It is not uncommon that people with BED stop enjoying activities they liked before, or become more isolated than before (willingly). In some extreme cases, it can happen that a person who spends enormous amounts of money on food starts shoplifting, and if the feeling of depression becomes too strong, it might even lead to self-harm.

Physical Aspects of Binge Eating Disorder

When it comes to physical symptoms, they can be spotted on different body-parts and in different stages. We will point out some of the most frequent ones in the following paragraphs.

On a mental level (brain) the symptoms are shown through self-esteem issues, food focus, and anxiety, which have already been mentioned.

But physically visible head symptoms are in a person's mouth. So you can spot a swollen jaw for example, or tooth decay, which often means bad breath too. The symptoms can also be having gum disease or erosion of a person's dental enamel.

The throat, on the other hand, will show the signs of heartburn and reflux, or will be inflamed. The symptoms can include chronic sore throat or esophagus rupture too.

Physically, binge eating disorder can cause a slow heartbeat or irregular digestive problems. More serious heart issues are cardiac arrest and in rare cases even heart failure. Note that heart issues can cause low blood pressure and a person who has some of these signs often feels dizzy or faints frequently.

People who have binge eating disorder often have problems with their stomachs too. They often feel pain and cramps, and they can suffer from stomach ruptures, diarrhea or constipation, and they have issues with their bowels and ulcers.

It is not unusual that people who suffer from BED to have irregular hormones. Women frequently have problems with their periods, which can lead to infertility.

Kidneys are often suffering from dehydration due to the amounts of food and the saltiness of food.

The skin of people with BED is often dry and they can have calluses on their knuckles.

One of the most common physical problems for people who have BED is their muscles. Frequently, the main cause is obesity, but anyhow, they usually suffer from lethargy and tiredness. Additionally, they often have cramps that are the product of imbalance in their electrolyte levels.

What Causes Eating Problems?

One of the most frequent theories is that binge-eating disorder is a product of a desire to escape our self-awareness. According to this theory, those who develop binge eating disorder have a very high level of expectation and their standards are even higher. Additionally, they are very sensitive when they receive or perceive demands from other people. This means that when others demand something of the person with binge eating issues, and he or she fails to meet those demands, their self-view becomes unflattering and they start developing even stronger and aversive self-awareness patterns. They start being compulsively concerned by the way that others perceive them. That concern further evolves into emotional distress that usually doesn't come alone. It is followed by depression and anxiety that influences the self-esteem of the person with BED immensely. With all this going on inside their heads, people with binge eating issues want to escape this unpleasant state they are in.

In theory, one of the techniques they use is a type of "cognitive response", which involves attention narrowing. This is achieved by reacting only to the immediate environmental stimuli while avoiding any kind of meaningful thoughts in the process. When using this kind of cognitive response, a person with binge eating problems disengages all negative aspects of overeating and accepts an uncritical approach toward it. This way of perceiving leads the patient toward irrational beliefs they start fostering like normal behavior. Another name for this kind of perception is the "escape model", and it is used to justify binge eating in the mind of the person with this kind of eating disorder.

Overeating is not a new thing. It has been known to humans since the time of ancient Rome. Even in those times, there were orgiastic binges. Today, on the other hand, we have numerous feasts, especially during the holidays, where heavy eating is a social norm for personal enjoyment rather than because of an issue. Still, some people don't stop eating too much even if they become obese which can threaten their well-being on both a physical and psychological level. Pathological overeating in many conceptualizations is divided into several levels, going from binge eaters to those who suffer from bulimia nervosa. These overeating concepts differ in their eating amounts and compensatory behaviors after eating. Also, it is not unknown that the implications of these psychopathologies along with motivation and behavioral patterns are different. However, they do have one common characteristic and it is to eat large quantities of food in a short period.

According to scientists such as Abraham and Beaumont, Polivy and Herman, Ruderman and Williamson (their researches were conducted during the 1980s and the beginning of the 1990s), overeating is actually a consequence of dieting. According to them the appearance of those who lose control while eating is connected to caloric restriction. As you probably already know, the main reason for dieting is weight loss. However, in most cases, diets don't bring any long-term solutions, so those who use dieting usually end up losing weight for a short amount of time only. The increased number of diet failures comes from the fact that when a person starts overeating from time to time after the diet ends, it immediately cancels all the effects achieved with previous caloric restriction.

It is true that environmental factors that can cause overeating are known about but there is still not enough information on the processes that are involved in excessive eating. The scientists we mentioned before (Polivy and Herman along with Ruderman) mention several environmental factors, such as caloric preload, emotional distress, and cognitive persuasion. So, one point of view for the cause of binge eating disorder is that binge eating is a result of low self-awareness, and the reason for being self-aware on a lower level can be explained by a motivational shift.

We have already mentioned that there is a connection between bulimia nervosa and binge eating disorder and that these two eating disorders don't exclude one another. From a scientific point of view (studies from Polivy and Herman along with the studies of Olmsted, Rudennan, and Grace in the 1980s), the pathological need to overeat is stronger for those who suffer from bulimia nervosa. It is said that general agreement on discontinuity is achieved when it comes to a comparison between dieting of people who have bulimia nervosa, and those who have binge eating disorder.

Even though one can argue about the bulimic and dieter studies and their pathological differences, the main focus is still on binge eating disorder. However, we mentioned these studies because these groups are also considered to be binge eaters. It is useful to know that binge eating isn't just a problem that affects those who are obese and that it doesn't only have to be connected to one condition exclusively.

The reason we keep pointing out the different binge eating aspects is that some might refer to binge eating in the same way as ordinary overeating in the colloquial sense. We already mentioned holiday feasts as an example. Still, it would be wrong to generalize binge eating in that manner. Although there are some similarities between those who have BED and bulimia nervosa, there are psychopathological motivations that can be taken as a distinction between the two. In the context of celebration norms, there are no signs of chronic dieting restraints or psychological categories that cause BED, even though they don't have to be excluded.

Note that the main reason for overeating, in the context of binge eating disorder, is a cognitive response for two reasons: the first one is restrained eating (dieting) and the other is connected with self-awareness (that can eventually lead to dieting before BED develops).

We can say that one of the theories that can explain the cause of eating problems is called the "Escape Theory". It is a theory that claims that people will develop eating disorders to escape from their self-awareness. In the following paragraphs, we will try to explain this theory in more detail, and you will see how feelings like anxiety and depression can shift one's motivation towards overeating.

So, as we explained, the fundamental meaning of escape theory is that binge eating happens when a person feels a motivation shift and, because of that shift, attempts to escape from their own self-awareness.

In this context, people who develop eating problems in general, tend to feel burdened by their own self-image, so, naturally, they look for some kind of escape. For these people, self-esteem is not on the highest level and not only do they find it burdensome to think about themselves but difficult too. Still, it is not that simple to "turn off" self-awareness. So the brain does one interesting thing. It has a strategy of narrowing attention to only those stimuli that can be found in the environment around it, quickly at the time the need arises. This is described in Baumeister's study conducted in the early 1990s. According to him, that is the best way to lower the level of self-awareness and to stop yourself from thinking about various implications that your behavior implies. There is another relevant aspect of this theory and it is connected to a multiplicity of self-awareness and the activities that one has while lowering it.

Keep in mind that low levels of self-awareness are referring to limited awareness of sensation and movement in a particular moment. This awareness is also narrowed to certain motivations and it is precise and temporary. On the other hand, when we talk about higher levels of self-awareness, it is connected to implications and periods that are bigger, thus broader. Additionally, a higher level of self-awareness means that a person compares themselves with a large number of expectations and standards set by society. And if that happens, according to Baumeister, a person develops traits that are permanent and later implemented for a period longer than just the "present moment". Contrarily, when a person lowers the lever of its self-awareness, according to Wagner and Vallacher, there will be no need for comparison (at least not a meaningful one), so there is no need to form traits that are durable or in line with general standards.

When you are reduced to lower levels of awareness, you are more focused on body sensations, which means that your experiences are limited. Furthermore, that means that your actions are influencing only your muscles without influencing your thoughts about the possible consequences. On the contrary, when a person has an increased level of self-awareness, their experiences become constructs that have a deeper meaning and connect their doing with the possible outcomes. Using the same logic, we can say that unlike higher self-awareness that has a broader meaning, lower self-awareness can be seen as deconstructed awareness.

It is safe to assume that this shift from higher to lower awareness of self actually means that you can "remove" possible concerns and thoughts of outcome that you had before. When shifting between these levels, one becomes less concerned with the consequences and deconstructs events to their own advantage. It is a way to run away from the pressure of high demands, and a perfect chance to leave behind everything that felt threatening and burdening.

One of the approaches says that those who develop binge eating disorder actually have a hard time evaluating themselves against the demanding ideals and the high standards they are expected to meet. For them, these standards extend to even higher levels than for average people. Most of all, these strict demands are connected to the body shape they should have according to social standards (which is usually a thin body figure). This is also known as "the stigma of obesity". The reason why many people start dieting is that society at one point has made clear that overweight people are not desired. There are all kinds of evidence that can be found on the account of stigmatization of obese people, which is why those who have binge episodes don't feel accepted and they tend to use extreme diets to lose weight. So, according to this approach, the main goal of binge eaters and their dieting is to be accepted in their social communities.

Some studies say that in modern Western societies, obese people are often belittled because of their bodies. According to the research of De Jong and Kleck conducted in 1986, there are bodyweight stereotypes. And when one compares a thin and obese person, the one with more weight is immediately seen as someone who is not as intelligent as the thinner person. In this comparison, the psychological characteristics of the person who has more weight are that he or she is shy and lonely (because fewer people choose obese people for friends). That person is perceived by society as someone who wants affection so badly that it is even labeled as greedy in that manner, and more importantly, that person is often seen as dependent on others. This is a classic stereotype that has been around since the mid-1980s.

The social rejection of overweight people was visible in multiple aspects and it was described and researched by many in the medical field. Being overweight doesn't have to mean that you need to be prejudiced with any of the traits mentioned above. Still, since there are still many people who share this kind of attitude, it is easy to influence the self-confidence of a person who is already sensitive because of the way he or she looks.

When it comes to women, it is more frequent that their eating habits are influenced by cultural standards and the way that society perceives them. This is the first level of their influence; the second level is their own internalized attitude about appropriate appearance. For women, more than for men, it was always far more important to have desirable figures, and if that's not the case, they frequently end up having trouble with their confidence and self-image in general.

For example, most women who suffer from bulimia have ended up with severe health consequences because they were afraid to become obese. This fear went so far that some of them felt overweight even if they didn't have any weight issues and they were even thin by average female weight standards.

It is even said that a lot of average women want to have less weight and even less than any man wants them to have. And, not surprisingly, this kind of attitude is frequent among those women who have eating disorders (including binge eating). The main motivation for them is a desire to have body shapes that they believe are proper shapes when compared with the preferences of men and other members of society. Nevertheless, we can say that eating problems are usually associated with body standards that are difficult or sometimes even too exaggerated to meet.

We would point out that before the beginning of the 20th-century, the fuller figure was actually a sign of beauty, especially for women. Seller connects this phenomenon with Venus, the love goddess, and that figure that was always presented with curves. However, when idolization of thin women started to emerge at the beginning of the 20th century, it had a huge impact on both society's standards and the attitude of women. According to some approaches, the reason why this shift from a fuller to thinner figure happened was that the classes of higher social standards started to look for new youth concepts and health notions. Generally speaking, it was simply a strong need to look at slim bodies rather than the rounder ones. This attitude eventually led to prejudicial behavior against those who were having weight issues and were obese.

Some argued that eating disorders were affecting more women because they were more targeted by society with the request of having preferred physiques. Once that women are surrounded by the attitude that being beautiful means that you must be thin they accept it as the opinion of others and social standardization that is supposed to be met. From a young age, many women receive an education (both formal and non-formal) that says how physical traits can help them acquire social status and above all interest from men (especially potential husbands). Well, the escape theory explains that eating problems along with dieting (because dieting is also perceived as an eating problem) mostly appear among people who are living in environments that force high body standards (thin body shape). That is why many eating disorders appears when there is a strong requirement for a specific body type.

As we mentioned, the escape model is one of the approaches that emphasize all relevant standards of being slim and turning to diet when it comes to binge eating disorder. Also, we have explained in more detail why high standards can cause a motivational shift and lead to binge eating in the first place. Still, we can't say that high body shape standards are the only reason for developing binge eating disorder. We focus more on women who have BED because there are more women than men affected by this problem. Another reason that one can start having eating problems is when a woman becomes (or wants to become) a high-achieving individual. Some statistics show how, for example, those who study medicine have more chances of developing eating disorders than those who study arts. Also, eating disorders are more frequent among those who are pursuing a career success, which is connected to high expectations in the business world. So, even these kinds of expectations that are very difficult to meet can be a cause of an eating problem.

So, we can say that most people who develop eating disorders such as bulimia or binge eating disorder are usually motivated by extremely high expectations and performance that they have trouble meeting. Many researchers (Mizer and Katzman among them) wrote about irrational standards and demands for approval that are unrealistic to meet. Both of these criteria are closely connected to those who have eating problems such as BED and bulimia. To review, there are three main reasons why people start having eating problems that we discussed until now. The first one is that eating disorders appear when there are standards and expectations too high to meet. The second is that those who want to meet demands related to body thinness becomes too extreme, and the third is related to the fact that these extreme eating patterns don't have to be related to physical appearance, they can also be a product of high career aspirations of individuals.

One of the basic premises of the escape model is that unrealistic standards lead to bad self-image when one starts comparing himself or herself with others (who, of course, meet those standards). The result of that comparison is that a person becomes unsatisfied and deficient. Binge eaters in this context are seen as people who have low self-esteem but they have a high aversion toward themselves and they tend to focus a lot of attention on it. You can look at it from two points of view. The first view is about self-image and the motivation behind negative self-view while the second point of view is more connected to self-attention and why certain focuses are higher than others (something like self-dislike). DeJong and Kleck point out that being obese doesn't provide pleasant feelings, and they define it with the following sentence: "The perception that one is overweight is a highly aversive state, particularly for females".

Note that having a dislike to your body doesn't automatically mean that you have an eating disorder. Many average women have problems accepting their bodies even if they are not overweight (they just think they are), and they even end up disliking themselves and their physical looks. Many cases suggest that the cause of eating disorders can vary and that they are mostly connected to negative body evaluation, especially among women. This kind of self-image is often followed with low confidence and esteem levels, thus way lower than it should be, even if there is no real reason for it. This is particularly true for those who have a bulimic eating disorder or those who tend to diet often.

Researchers such as Bauer and Anderson, or Butterfield and LeClair have identified that most of those who have eating disorders view themselves as failures, thus defining this kind of attitude as the major cause of eating disorder tendency. For those with eating problems, even those who are treated as failures without being connected to weight issues have an impact on the body image that people with eating disorders have. Additionally, these negative views influence unhealthy eating patterns that are common among everyone that suffers from an eating disorder regardless of its type.

According to one of the many laboratory studies done on this topic, those who had lower self-esteem while dieting ended up eating much more ice-cream than those who were dieting and having higher self-esteem. Also, when manipulations were done on all these participants, the result was overeating. For example, when those with lower self-esteem received information that they didn't solve a task they increased the number of their meals regardless of their diet rules. The same thing happened once they found out that they had to have a performance in front of an audience that will be evaluating them. The amount of food got bigger, without dieting restraints. This means that binge eating is actually a product of being self-aware but in an aversive way. Furthermore, escape theory suggests that this aversive feeling comes from a comparison between one's self and the standards he or she considers relevant.

Therefore, we can say that the feeling of self-awareness is at the beginning and is really heightened among those who have binge eating disorder.

There is an interesting scale, invented during the 1980s, by Herman and Policy that measures eating behaviors that are restrained. This scale shows a correlation with the scale of self-consciousness invented three years later. According to the correlation of these two scales, chronic eating behaviors are directly connected with how the person with an eating disorder thinks it appears to others. Note that there is also a scale that measures self-focus and it was used for the first time in 1977. When using these scales, those who didn't have restrained eating regiments had a normal self-focus level while those who were using restrained eating patterns tended to have self-focus that was more egocentric. Some of the examined participants even showed psychopathic signs. When comparing the bulimia test and restraint scale, the study showed that the result of certain individuals was closely connected to Narcissistic personality disorder (NPD). All these scale correlations concluded that those who are using restricting eating patterns have a strong self-focus, thus self-preoccupation.

Until now, we have discussed how high standards and self-awareness that suggests a failure in meeting these standards are the strongest causes of binge eating disorder and eating problems in general. The aversive feelings towards one's self come from the awareness that a person has shortcomings that they are unable to correct. This feeling frequently creates a negative effect, therefore it becomes a strong motivation for escape. Negative effects are evidential and are shown in different states of a person with binge eating disorder. One of the most common negative effects is depression. It is even more frequent among those suffering from the bulimic disorder. Multiple studies connect clinical depression with bulimia. You can read more about it in the works of Delvin and Walsh, or Mitchel and Eckert. Additionally, Hinz, Williamson, Lease, Fitcher, Rusell, and many others wrote about correlations between depression and eating disorders.

In some reviews, statistics showed that up to 77% of those who have eating disorders experience at least some kind of affective disorder. Another correlation that was established at the end of the 20th century is that depression was connected to restraint eating. During the 1990s, it was proven that most of those who were dieting had higher scores on a depression inventory made by Beck in the 1960s. This result was much higher than with those who had normal eating patterns. We would like to point out that the study also showed how "depressed mood and self-deprecating thoughts follow binge eating". This was one of the criteria used to diagnose this eating disorder. Also, the thing that was established later is that those who were dieting and becoming clinically depressed tended to gain more and more weight once they started eating. On the contrary, those who didn't do any dieting started losing weight when faced with depression.

When it comes to anxiety as one of the main reasons for having eating problems, it is clear that it has a big influence on binge eaters. Anxiety is primarily connected with the way that social groups accept those who suffer from eating disorders. This is especially significant when people start to feel rejected or excluded. According to many, these are the main reasons why people dealing with BED (and other eating disorders) tend to get anxious. The fear of rejection is strong and one of the key features in all eating disorders. Since we are always mentioning bulimia along with binge eating (because of their complex connection), anxiety is considered to be the main reason behind developing this disorder along with binge eating. One of the definitions says that it " derives from an unfulfilled craving for nurturance and a remedy for intensely painful feelings of rejection and loneliness".

Desire to be thin can lead to eating problems, and the main reason why there is this kind of desire in the first place is the fear that otherwise an individual will be rejected by their social group. Another reason can be a criticism of physical looks or negative evaluation of the latter. On the other hand, social anxiety is connected to all eating disorders, but even more with those that involve dieting.

Usually, those who have eating problems have general emotional distress too. The escape model is based on the premise that when a person with an eating problem responds to produce distress, they have more emotions than the person without any eating issues.

There is a way of periodic self-monitoring that can help a person to track the eating pattern and the mood while having a binge episode (if having one). Some people with eating disorders feel lonelier than the others, but during the binge episode, one can show a negative mood that is even more heightened than normal. Many questionnaires can help a person examine if they have eating problems. It is possible to actually follow a binge episode, and what was established on several occasions was that during a binge episode mood tends to be much more negative than usual. However, binge eaters are not the worst. Bulimic people have more negative moods than binge eaters. The important point of the role of emotional distress is that there is an emotional trigger that activates binge episodes.

The question that arises in all these situations is why each time when they feel some kind of stress, people with eating problems tend to overeat? Well, one of the most frequent explanations is that overeating or binge episodes help them regulate their bad mood and relieves them temporarily. For those who have bulimia and engage themselves in binge episodes, that feeling is satisfaction is just for a moment. There are several reasons why that can happen, it might feel like they have achieved something, or like they escaped from something. There are many different attitudes about this still, it was established that mood satisfaction can't be the only reason that maintains binge episodes, thus binge eating disorder in general.

Still, it has been proven that binge episodes reduce anxiety and that the biggest distress happens at the moment before eating. So, anxiety reduction may be a direct consequence of binge eating. Still, there is a danger that an increased amount of distress can impact control mechanisms for eating and that the larger number of situations causing distress happens, the overeating will increases too and it will lead to interferences between control and overeat simultaneously. Note that negative experiences and mood can also be a consequence of an unsuccessful diet or something similar.

So, the real question now is the role of distress. Distress is a feeling that keeps a person thinking about how dieting is not important and that it is not obtainable for him or her in the first place. A person who has a binge-eating problem starts exercising routine patterns and narrowing the scope of their attention, it will lead it toward the reduction of concerns and insecurities. In this scenario, binge episodes are actually a strategy, a mechanism to focus all attention on one thing, thus removing all other issues from the picture. This kind of escape has a few additional contexts that can be explained. Firstly, overeating is promoted as a pleasure in the eyes of the person who has lost control of their eating pattern. It represents a short distraction from the real issues and it alleviates depression and anxious feelings. However, it doesn't last long so it is inevitable that binge episodes become repetitive.

Although we dedicated a lot of time to emotional distress as one of the main factors for binge eating, it doesn't mean that all forms of distress will cause this disorder. For example, if someone is experiencing physical feat, it won't trigger binge episodes, unlike previous examples of depressive and anxiety states. That's where ego and negative mood threats come into play. If you cause these kinds of feelings, it will definitely activate a binge episode. Still, it doesn't mean that the person will immediately lose control of themselves.

There is a huge difference between those who use different kinds of diets and those who didn't. Those who did had more difficulty with controlling their binge episodes and they responded to different stimulators such as ego threats with binge episodes, frequently without control. On the other hand, those who didn't have the opportunity to diet had a stronger sense of control and they showed fewer changes when confronted with some kind of stressful situation. We can say that self-evaluation is a key factor here, which is why it should be carefully nurtured, especially if you have a tendency of developing some kind of eating problem. When confronting feelings of distress and physical fear, it is evident that fear can't cause the type of stress that leads to eating problems, while distress certainly can.

We can conclude that emotional distress is one of the main factors that cause eating problems, especially binge eating disorder. Anxiety and depression are also strong factors; however, they are even stronger when it comes to bulimia nervosa and anorexia as two other common types of eating problems or eating disorders. The most frequent combination that triggers binge eating disorder is distress infused with self-esteem threats. In the end, eating problems might occur as a response to stress or bad mood if they are perceived as temporal pain alleviation.

Binge Eating and Addiction

Binge eating disorder is considered to be addictive because it represents a way of dealing with issues in life just like some people tend to turn to alcohol, medications or drugs. The best way to understand this is to approach binge eating psychologically. However, even if there are differences with psychological symptoms and physical characteristics of eating disorders and their addictive behavior, all of them share the same psychological aspect of having underpinnings. Some definitions claim that environmental drive is another common characteristic along with low self-esteem. All eating disorders (even though we focus primarily on binge eating) have an accent on the body size, and while they might seem different in some aspects, they are all equally addictively strong and bad for the health.

Addiction is defined as a way of obtaining emotional satisfaction. It is said that addiction provides a sense of life control, love and security, but that the effects are temporary and treated like an illusion. When an addict figures out that solution wasn't a long-term one, he/she starts having an even stronger feeling of disgust towards themselves. Their coping mechanisms become weaker and the feeling of security is reduced to a minimum. These kinds of feelings are common for all addictions, and binge eating disorder is no exception.

One can argue that this addictive behavior has the clearest circle in the case of binge eating disorder because it points to the simplest yet most effective nature of an addict who feeds their negative emotions.

It is a self-feeding with a negative relationship, and that relationship is the one that the mentioned addict has with food.

Of course, many other things are defined as addictive behavior. Nowadays addiction can refer to games, gambling, pornography, and many other activities that all kinds of people do in certain patterns. They all have this resemblance in repeating a certain operation to achieve a certain emotional satisfaction. The same principle applies to binge eating along with other eating disorders we mentioned before. The reason why food addiction is not recognized as an official addiction is the fact that psychiatry in the USA has rules of deciding when something is addictive or not. It is like creating a drug list for example. This means that eating disorders will have to undergo an unknown number of contortions that will decide if there is enough reason to declare eating disorders along with binge eating as addictions. Still, for now, there is at least "substance use" as one of the official addictions on the list, so hopefully, over time, this will evolve into sub-categories that will include BED.

The Treatment of Binge Eating Disorder

The main types of therapies used in binge eating disorder treatment are psychological and behavioral therapies.

The most famous one is known as Cognitive behavioral therapy or CBT for short. This is a type of psychotherapy that has a goal of observing and defining relationships that a person develops in their thoughts. What kind of feelings and behaviors is that person using? What caused them? And how to reduce negativity and replace previous behavior patterns with the more desirable ones. Cognitive-behavioral therapy can be led by a therapist, it can be held individually or in a group. Additionally, it can be done as a structured and guided self-help too.

In a therapy led by a therapist, the goal is to provide education during each session whether it is an individual or a group. The main task of the therapist is to teach those who have BED useful skills and to support their patients during the whole recovery process. There is another type of a therapist-led CBT, it is a treatment partially led by the therapist, as its name suggests. The goal of this kind of treatment is to leave a person with BED to watch videos that are highly educational and then talk about the video during the session when the therapist actually appears.

The third type of cognitive-behavioral therapy that we mentioned is called the structured self-help, and it represents a therapy where instead of the therapist, the person with BED gets the manual. The manual is written to lead the session just as the therapist is really there, and the main task of the person on the treatment is to read the manual. If in the group, after the video, the discussion would be led by a group member rather than the therapist.

There are some additional types of psychotherapy that can be useful to know:

Intrapersonal psychotherapy, also known as IPT is a therapy that has a goal of helping the person with BED realize the social aspect of developing this disorder and why binge eating represents a coping mechanism. The main reason why this kind of therapy works is that helps those with BED to deal with all kinds of negative emotions that are produced by failed social interactions. It is useful for increasing intrapersonal skills among other things.

Another useful therapy is dialectical behavior therapy or DBT for short. It is a therapy that represents one of the most recent forms of cognitive-behavioral therapy and is designed specifically for behaviors that are considered to be impulsive. DBT along with IPT represents a support treatment and it is very useful in terms of research.

Lastly, in recent years, there is another method that helped a lot of people dealing with binge eating disorder, and it is known as mindfulness-based eating awareness training or MB-EAT for short. This is not a psychotherapy method. However, it has proven to be very efficient. It blends strategies about mindful eating that help people deal concretely with their eating patterns.

Of course, there are all sorts of medications that can be used while dealing with BED. Still, keep in mind that even though we offer some concrete list of medications that can help, you shouldn't use them before consulting with a doctor.

The reason we were pointing to the help of at least a pharmaceutical worker is the fact that the first group of medications that are widely used among people who have different eating disorders is antidepressants. The most frequently used ones are known as SSRIs or selective serotonin reuptake inhibitors. The reason they are recommended is that several studies have shown that they can reduce the number of binge episodes. Additionally, antidepressants have a huge impact on feelings of depression, which is the reason they were made in the first place.

Another type of medication that is used for binge eating disorder is from the group of ADHD medications and it is called Vyvanse. This is also the first medication that was approved for BED treatment (by The FDA-food and drug administration). It was proven that this medicine can reduce binge episodes per week and that it can influence compulsive behavior when it comes to food. Another medicine that was also tested was Topirimate from the group of anti-convulsing medications. However, its usefulness is very limited.

Although there are medicines that got approval for treating binge eating disorder, there are still potential side-effects of all medication used for treatment. On the other hand, there isn't any psychotherapy method that can have such risks. Please keep in mind that the best way to decide which method of treatment will help you is to discuss it with a doctor, especially if you insist on taking medication.

Diets-Calorie Restriction, Low-Fat Diets, Low-Carb, Diets - DON'T Work

Carbohydrates are known to raise blood sugar levels, so when low-carb diets appeared for the first time, they were very well accepted in contrast to high carb and low-fat diets that were popular before that. One of the most famous low-carb diets is known as the Atkins' diet. This kind of diet is popular because it allows you to eat different kinds of food (like bacon for example) and still lose weight. Still, this "long-lasting" and "quick" effect that was promised wasn't as successful as it was believed. On the other hand, many people were impressed by the fact that they could eat and lose weight really fast. It often seemed like the kinds of food in low-carb diets would help with some health issues like cholesterol. When the Atkins' diet was first released in 1972, it was said that the diet helped with chronic disease, but that is far from the truth because soon enough the downsides of these types of diets were visible.

All low-carb diets based on the Atkins' diet don't have the desired effect, without exception. There was a study done in 2018 that says how all its participants lost the same amount of weight using diets that are based on low carb principles. Still, the consequences of low-carb food lifestyle can be serious, and in most of the cases, the diet isn't even functional long-term, and your health might suffer at one point. This is especially important when you deal with obesity or being overweight. Low-carb diets might do a little good for cutting carbohydrates, still, their shortage produces big chaos in your body. The point is that when your body starts using muscles (the body mass) for energy, your metabolism slows down. The reason for that is muscle tissue that burns up calories to work better which is one of the main reasons why many of those who stop eating according to a diet start having binge eating episodes, start gaining weight again, and it often comes back very quickly, even double. And returning weight is not the biggest issue. These diets can impact the cardiovascular system.

When your metabolism slows down, your body breaks. This happens because muscles burn up a lot of calories, and it is probably one of the reasons why weight starts coming back when you shun carbs for any length of time. Switching to a diet that allows you to eat a lot of meat but restricting many other things can raise your cholesterol. This causes an amino acid called homocysteine level to rise, which means that it increases the possibility of getting heart disease.

Low-carb diets require you to give up fruit, bread, and many other things. It is an extreme calorie restriction that can really influence your binge eating later. The feeling of deprivation will become stronger and the body will crave nutrients and other food that is essential to its functioning. In combination with emotions such as anxiety, stress, and depression, this can quickly lead back to binge episodes.

Another reason why low-carb diets don't work is that because they include eating a lot of "bad" fat. Although diets such as the Atkins diet are popular because they allow eating food that is forbidden in most other diets (cheeseburgers for example), it is still an extremely restricting way of eating. In the last few years, there have been variations that included a few healthier ingredients. However, when we talk about what really happens after you stop eating fruit, beans, bread, and many other things, it becomes very easy to get accustomed to fast food, and if you load a lot of fat into your body, it will impact your health because it can seriously increase LDL cholesterol levels. Even if bacon and butter sound tempting at the beginning, these diets are not good in the long run because once you stop eating strictly by their rules, you risk gaining even more weight. More importantly, you risk your health.

Reaching the energy balance is something that even nutritionists can't tell 100% accurately. To reach a certain weight goal more healthily is often about the fact that a person has to learn how to let the energy in and release it out. "Practicing" this balance with diets is something that doesn't really work well when you start restricting calories, especially if these restrictions are extremely high. The technology has evolved, but not to the point where it can calculate with certainty the number of calories we had per meal or per day. And if there is a difference between the number of calories that we took and the amount that was calculated, it is impossible to know how much we'd have to burn off. One of the reasons why calorie restriction isn't good is that this gap that is potentially happening represents a difference that can make you either thin or really obese in a matter of a few years. Additionally, there is another question that arises. If the number of calories was that significant for body weight, how was it possible to deal with bodyweight management before there was even a concept of calories known worldwide? In comparison, it's like trying to lower the level of CO_2 in the body with a fast breathing technique. It is efficient for a few minutes, and that's all.

Much research shows that the real reason why conventional diets don't work is the countermeasures that the organism launches when we cut out something that it needs. In many cases, this is highly disregarded which is why cutting calories is still one of the main methods that people suffering from obesity and eating disorders use to lose weight. The body is powerful, and when it feels that it lacks something, it releases countermeasures that will slow down or completely stop weight loss. This means that the more you want to lose weight and more things you deny eating, your body wants it even more badly than before, and it fights back.

Let's return to more classic studies like before. In the 1980s, Rockefeller University in New York made a study in which its research had volunteers for weight loss. After reducing their weight by 20% they were examined for their metabolism regardless of their body weight at the beginning of the study. What was found was that no matter if the participant was obese or not, after restricting calories to lose weight, they all had the same metabolic problem- its rate was dropping and it was more because of the way of losing weight than the weight loss alone. The side effect was the fact that these strict food regiments caused more binge eating because all who participated felt hungrier and hungrier.

Restricting calories, and dieting, in general, leads to failure in most cases. This is a concept known to anyone who has been using strict food regiments: the fewer calories the body receives the more efficiently it will burn them. But slowing down metabolism while the hunger rises is a combination that leads to bad results every time. When a person who has any kind of eating problem starts depriving himself for days and weeks, the temptation becomes very strong, even stronger than normal. Also, there is a big chance that health consequences will start even before the weight reduction. The constant feeling of being tired and sleeping too much can lead to stronger temptation to quit these routines, stay in bed, and eat everything in sight. However, if a person goes through with the diet and starts losing weight, the other side of the story is that the metabolism will keep slowing down.

This principle of the body's self-regulation is also true when people don't have weight issues at all. The same Rockefeller research had volunteers who weren't obese and they were forced to gain weight while being monitored. They were gaining weight and their metabolism was really fast, but at one point, more and more volunteers started losing interest in food in general. This led to the end of enforced eating and their bodies worked until the body weight was the same as before the testing.

Note that it is difficult to change body weight regardless of trying to gain weight or to lose it. Losing 40 pounds is extremely difficult, but gaining 40 pounds is hard too. The point is that in both cases (under-eating and overeating) the body responds. IT wants to return the body to the starting point or so-called "set point". This starting weight point is something that is often determined by our genes. Being a binge eater and trying to restrict all sorts of food will only make things worse. The same concept applies to those who are obese not only thanks to their eating problems but due to their parents' genes.

Being less healthy and less effective than originally claimed is a principle that can be applied to low-fat diets too. The reason why we mentioned genes as one of the reasons why the struggle to lose weight can be even more difficult is because there is another opinion that explains how eating habits developed in a family are far more important for dealing with weight issues. As you know, binge eating is a disorder that most frequently has obesity or overweight as a result of frequent binge episodes. Nowadays obesity is a serious problem in the United States. It is believed that the high-fat diet was one of the strongest factors in developing obesity. The common belief of people in each society is that if you eat a lot of fat you will have a lot of fat. It would be logical to think that eating more fatty food more frequently would help you gain weight, but that is not entirely true. David Ludwig from Harvard's medical school conducted research in which it was explained why low-fat diets aren't the answer. It is also an excellent study that talks about the real reasons why obesity is so frequent in American society. It is said that the numbers that were shown by 2010 pointed out that eating disorders and obesity as their product, don't necessarily mean that that is a genetic heritage. Actually, in Harvard's study that we mentioned above, it is claimed that it is not.

The Journal of the American Medical Association is a study in which another expert, Dr Willett, explains studies that have been conducted on real body fat and dietary fat. What was determined was that the major determinant of body fat is not dietary fat. Another proof that low-fat diets won't help you lose weight, this won't help you with your binge eating problem was a clinical trial done by The Women's Health Initiative. It published the result of 50,000 females of different ages and cultures losing no weight while implementing a low-fat diet. Other studies have shown that there are huge differences between those who follow different kinds of diet food regimen (low-carb, calorie reduction, low fat), but the outcome is the same- health issues and weight return after you stop following it. According to Harvard's study, it is evident that various diets will produce various effects, and that it is not possible to treat obesity if we don't have a personalized plan for anyone suffering from obesity and eating disorder along with it. According to Ludwig, there is a whole new part of science that can be used to explain how food can be used to fight mental and physical signs and aspects of having obesity issues.

The body of those who underwent changes for the studies we mentioned above was observed for belly fat and waist circumference and not only for its weight. What was found was that those who had higher insulin secretors had more chance of having belly fat than those who had lower levels. Additionally, it was found that those who had higher insulin secretors tended to have a bigger possibility of influencing their weight and that their chances were much better than for those who have lower insulin. Now, when people who have a high insulin level started losing weight using low-fat diets, the results were not good. The reason for this is simple: insulin does two things to our organism. The first one is that it makes you hungry even more than you would normally be, and the other is that it helps to produce more fat-storage hormone. When having increased fat-storage hormone, belly fat increases which are why low-fat diets, besides being unhealthy, are not the wisest choice.

When the study was made, it was established that people who had higher insulin secretors also had bigger changes in their weight. It was also determined that people who had lower insulin secretors did better with low-fat diets.

For example, when you increase the level of carbohydrates your insulin increases and you become hungry. Logically, the thing you crave is to eat more carbs and usually sugar. Another thing that happens and it is especially bad for the people who have BED is that after the insulin level increases, the desire for eating is stronger during the whole day.

Some of the things that your organism might need and crave for but diets usually don't have in their eating menus are as the following:

- vegetables, fruit and whole grains that can help

you with strokes, preventing heart diseases, getting diabetes, prevent cancer and fighting to develop metabolic syndrome typical of those who frequently diet. Fruit is known to have fewer calories and some of them can be very filling. Both fruit and vegetables are healthy alternatives that are usually not included in low carb and fat diets.

- beans are another thing that the body might crave. They are full of vitamins, protein, and carbohydrates. They are rich in fiber and they don't have "bad" fat. Apart from that, beans produce chemicals that can help with the prevention of heart disease so keep that in mind while planning your meals.

Using a carb-restricted diet means that the body will often lack protein and calcium. When the body starts craving these nutrients, the best way to satisfy that craving is to look for fat-free milk or yogurt products.

Reducing health risks includes consuming a sufficient amount of fiber too. The body will often crave it and the best thing is that in most cases it is already inside some other foods (like the vegetables and fruit we mentioned above). Craving fiber means that potentially your body reacts to low blood pressure, LDL cholesterol or a low level of blood sugar. Another thing you should be aware of is that no matter which of these diets you considered trying, they are not really a solution to any of your problems. You will not get the results that you want, at least not long-term. Deprivation usually leads to even stronger binge episodes so think carefully about the way you want to deal with the problem. Also, diets rarely provide enough vitamins and minerals. As a matter of fact, many diets point out that the person dieting by a certain diet pattern should take vitamin supplements, otherwise it can affect their health badly.

Ignoring our hunger Signals Results in Food Obsession and Often Binge Eating Later

Hunger is not something that we can call failure or blame only diets for it. There is a whole science behind the fact that someone is hungry when being denied a certain food. One of the main issues is connected to the stigma that follows eating disorders too. When people say ''binge eating disorder'' they often consider that binging is the main cause of obesity and that this and other eating disorders are the first lines if having weight issues. Still, it would be more accurate to say that different kinds of attempts to regulate weight (diets) are often the cause of binging, to begin with.

When you are deprived of some food, the natural response of your body would be to crave that food and overeating or binging at some point isn't the worst possible thing to happen, but the most normal reaction. Our basic instinct is self-preservation, and our bodies are made so they can protect themselves if there is a possibility of starvation. When the body feels threatened by a lack of food, it releases a large number of hormones that result in making you even hungrier than you were in the first place. It also leads to the feeling of getting full slower to extend the food search. A need to eat in these situations is not a cause of a disorder but a natural biological reaction to restriction.

Nowadays, there is a popular expression used for overeating or binging after dieting and it is labeled yo-yo dieting. If a person diets often, the body feels like it is in crisis all the time, it loses support from nutrients and spends calories that were stored for safety. This further leads to hormone release that becomes more and more effective and they are sending a signal to us that we should eat. The stronger the restriction the bigger hunger one feels. This leads to eating large amounts of food in a short time, thus the direct consequence is a binge episode. At first, binging is a normal reaction to this kind of situation. However, as we have already explained, at some point, binging can become a disorder that has to be struggled with.

Focusing On Weight Instead Of Health and Nutrition Is Not Helpful and Actually Can Lead Us to Unhealthy Behavior

Some dietary patterns or diets are designed to be more "prudent" than others. They include vegetables and fruit, sometimes even whole grains. It is said that they can help to resolve weight issues long term. On the other hand, there are more "Western" diets that promote meat, sweets and another kind of carbohydrates. But the point of both diet approaches is that they are still health risks, which means that there is a possibility of developing diabetes, heart issues, and many other chronic conditions.

There are diets defined such as "The Mediterranean"

and "The American" diet, and they both have their own ways of gaining body weight control and regulating it. For example, most of the fat used in Mediterranean diets comes from olive oil and other plants while American diets mostly have food focused on bigger calorie numbers. Fish, fruit, and beans are also included in diets nowadays and they do help you to lose weight but only temporarily.

The main point is that losing weight is not the only objective when suffering from an eating disorder. Rather than that, it is far more important to focus on eating healthier and prevent your body from releasing hormones that will make you hungry again. And the best way to stop the body from releasing the "hungry" hormones is to make it happy.

For example, most of the studies claim how breakfast is one of the most important meals of the day and how skipping it can increase obesity risk. But the kind of breakfast matters too. Also, it is important to keep track of snacks and the frequency of meals. Having multiple meals and snacks during the day might seem like something that won't help with dealing with binge eating disorder, but it is not true because if the ingredients are healthy, the frequency can be even useful.

If we focus only on our weight loss rather than our health it can backfire on us. For example, if you use strict food regiments and you end up "loosening up" for a celebration or something, you can end up with larger portions, fast food or unhealthy amounts of different kinds of food. And if you are dieting often and you have these episodes more and more, it can end up becoming a habit that can easily lead up to BED. And if you already fight eating disorders such as binge eating, focusing on weight loss is a wrong strategy, to begin with. The obesity from this disorder is often caused by behavior we mentioned above – restriction and "breaks" from overeating. The point is that you have to determine the real reason behind binge eating and then start focusing on the change that you have to make. And more diets won't help with that. On the contrary, your body will release more hormones, and you can still suffer from some serious health issues. Of course, one of the goals should be to reduce weight if that will raise your self-confidence. However, a healthier way to deal with this kind of problem is to think about it really hard and try to accept that body shape is not all there is to a human's looks. Being healthy is far more important than looking good. Society has its own issues and many emotions caused by social standards were indeed the reason why binge eating started happening in the first place. Still, the restriction is not the key to weight loss at the cost of your health.

Another thing that you should be aware of is the role of fast food. Many people turn to fast food because it is cheap, the portions are often large and it has high amounts of sugar. Since most people nowadays work intensively, and a lot of adolescents eat outside of the house, it is no wonder why fast food became one of the main causes of obesity and being overweight. People with binge episodes tend to eat fast food because it is accessible and it can satisfy cravings. On the other hand, when considering reducing weight it is recommended to avoid fast food, but for the person who does overtime and doesn't have the time to prepare food at home and money to buy healthy food from the restaurant, this means starvation until they finish their jobs. As you can see, this is not a solution either. Staying hungry for too long can cause dizziness, it certainly causes the feeling of being tired, and hence, it influences your productivity. If you are not satisfied, and furthermore you feel hungry all the time, the natural course of events is that at one point binge episodes will happen again. Your health will be at risk from being hungry all the time, you won't be happy at all, and at the end of the day, you won't be able to control your weight the way you want to.

The bottom line is that if you eat healthier and, of course, pay attention to what you eat, you can prevent both health issues such as chronic disease and manage your weight better.

Chapter 3

Manage Hunger In 9 Moves

Managing hunger can be a challenging task, however, here are seven ways you can help yourself avoid overeating.

1) Keep Hunger under Control - 5 Snack Techniques

Five snack techniques refer to the way you can help yourself get from one meal to another and avoid binge episodes. We would say that in this context, having a snack is a must if you aim to fight an eating problem. The good thing about snacks is that, if you choose the right ones and eat them at the right time, you won't hear your stomach rumbling and you won't have a problem with your energy. This is especially important if you work at an intensive and stressful job. So the secret of the 5-snack technique revolves around the right ingredients that can help fight the binge.

On many diets, snacks are seen as something bad. However, snacks can be seen as meals (or mini-meals to be precise), and they can be very useful to supplement the body with the nutrients it wasn't able to get from the meal. Also, if you have breaks between meals that are too long, the chance of having a binge episode increases radically.

Note that the best way to use snacks is to choose those that have up to 200 calories. Also, always make sure that you eat a snack whenever you have more than a three-hour pause between the meals. For most of the people with regular jobs, this means that the first snack should be between 10 a.m. and 3 p.m. because most often there are no lunch breaks at that time.

There are five snacks that you should start adding to your meal plan daily while making sure that you always eat them between meals or if you really feel that you will have another binge episode.

The first snack combines fiber, protein and lean protein, and it also provides you with a healthy amount of fat. That is everything you need for a healthy hunger satisfaction before regular meals. This snack is essentially peanut butter combined with whole-wheat crackers. The reason why this snack is great, especially for the first snack after breakfast (when normally the break between meals is the largest) is that fiber and proteins help you control your hunger while fat makes you feel full for a longer time since it needs more time to digest.

You can make this snack by using one tablespoon of peanut butter with 4 crackers (whole-wheat ones). And if possible, it would be best to have natural peanut butter. And if you want to keep track of your calories, this snack has approximately 180 calories.

Another snack that is actually more focused on getting you enough vegetables is a light veggie soup. If you have a warm cup of soup after a long day at work, you will feel like a new person. The reason why vegetable soup is highly recommended is that also has a lot of fiber, and fiber means that you will have a sensation of being full for a longer time. In practice, this means that your binge episode won't happen and that you will have a snack that will prevent increasing of the high blood sugar level for that day. Normal sugar level means that there will be no hunger pains and that you can spend the time without thinking about being hungry or overeating. You can change vegetables as needed, and let's say that you can try with bean soup. For those who keep track of their calorie intake, one cup of veggie soup contains 100 calories, which means that if you are really hungry, you can have up to two cups.

Another snack that you should consider for the day is fruit and low-fat cheese because it has a good protein balance. This combination of ingredients also contains fat (low level) and carbs, and when you add fibers that you get from the fresh fruit, it is a great combination for managing hunger. You can choose different fruits each day, one day you can eat pears, another day you can choose berries or pineapple, there is a wide choice. The advantage of this snack is that apart from helping you keep your hunger under control, it also provides you with additional calcium, which is useful for bones. For calorie-trackers, one portion (1/2 cup of cheese and ½ cup of fruit) has approximately 140 calories.

The fourth snack that is excellent in helping with hunger management is a combination of sliced vegetables and hummus that became very popular in recent years all around the world so it can be found in every store and for a good price. Hummus is a Middle-Eastern product and it is rich with fiber, fats, and protein. On the other hand, combining it with vegetables such as broccoli, carrots, and peppers, for example, makes it a great combination of nutrients that can satisfy hunger before it turns out into a binge episode. You can combine three tablespoons of hummus with one cup of sliced vegetables (you can choose a different kind each day) and you will get a snack that contains approximately 120 calories.

The last type of snack that we will talk about can be called a "trail mix" snack. It is a combination that contains peanuts, almonds, walnuts and so on. As you might suspect, they are all full of protein, fiber, and fat. Making a "trail mix" snack is quite simple, you just take a hand full of let's say nuts, and you mix them with dried fruit such as cranberries for example (use two tablespoons for dried fruits). Since nuts are known to be high in calories, you can reduce that number by choosing dry nuts. You can pack "trial mix" in a plastic bag or a cup, just as long as it is easy for you to grab it. The combination of two tablespoons of dried fruit and hand full of nuts (more or less 15 nuts) has approximately 170 calories.

All these snacks will help you manage your hunger during the day and will keep you full. A result is a reduced number of binge eating episodes caused by calorie reduction or dieting and a healthy intake of nutrients.

2) Raw Vegetables and Herbal Teas Come in Handy

Eating raw vegetables is considered to be healthy for various reasons. The first one is the belief that having food that is uncooked or unprocessed in any way can prevent many diseases (cancer and heart diseases among others). The other reason is that some approaches claim how cooking vegetables, and food in general, reduces the number of enzymes that can help our bodies absorb and digest nutrients that we need better.

Raw vegetables can be used on many occasions; they can be used for snacks as we explained in the previous section for example. Raw vegetables can be a great salad, they can be excellent for smoothies. You can use them to make all kinds of soups or to make a dressing for other healthy food that you decided to make. When dealing with eating disorders, staying healthy is the most important goal, more important than just losing weight and stopping binge eating episodes. That is why it is good to start making differences from the start. For instance, raw vegetables are not the same thing as frozen vegetables. Note that frozen vegetables have usually been boiled before frozen, thus they lose most of the properties that you need from raw vegetables.

As you can see, it is handy to have raw vegetables in the house at all times. There is a variety of choices to use. Additionally, you can even look for sea veggies if you want to try something more exotic.

Although they are not exactly vegetables, raw fruit, nuts, seeds, and grains are also an excellent source of nutrients that you need. For example, there are a large number of dishes or snacks that you can use fruit for. They can be dried, whole, fresh, used in smoothies, juices, for making powders, all kinds of mixes and so on. Nuts and seeds are also good to use them for pesto, butter, to make creams and eat them as meals (chia seed for example) in combination with non-fat yogurt. Grains, such as rice, are actually plant produced and you can use these in combination with raw vegetables and make a lot of delicious dishes that are highly nutritious and good for both hunger and weight management.

Drinking tea is basically like drinking medicine from a mug. Apart from the water, this is one of the most popular beverages in the world. However, keep in mind that ice-tea is not the same thing as brewed tea and that having a proper cup of warm tea can do you a lot of good, especially if you make it a substitute for commercial juices. Another important thing to note about tea is that most of the tea plants don't have caffeine. Herbal teas are full of nutrients and they are one of the healthiest beverages that you can use when you are dealing with binge eating disorder and eating problems in general.

Except for drinking, tea herbs can be used in dishes

and salads, and they can be a good addition to some smoothies (try adding mint or ginger to some of the smoothies you make). This means that you have two ways of using tea herbs- eat them and drink them, which is very handy and in most cases within your budget too. Here are a few of the most frequently used herbal teas that you should try.

The first one, called the Rooibos (in pronunciation it is Roy-boss) has a specific use for obesity prevention. It is native to South Africa since it is a leaf from the shrub tree. This tea is rich with compounds used to fight inflammation and it has a lot of antioxidants too. Another great benefit of this tea is that it is good for your bones and that it improves digestion. As you can see, one leaf, if used properly, can have an enormous influence on your body.

Chamomile is one of the most famous tea herbs since ancient times. In lore, and in many versions of folk medicine, there is a common main purpose for chamomile tea- to calm you and to make you sleep. However, there are some additional perks of chamomile, one of them being the protection of the density of bones and another common use of this flower is regulation of sugar level in blood.

We already mentioned ginger as a great additive to a lot of stuff you can make from fruit and vegetables whether you use it in food or in beverages. Ginger is known to help morning and motion sickness, and for ages, it has been used as a remedy for nausea. Different parts of the ginger plant have different benefits. The root of the ginger plant can help to fight strong inflammation that can be caused by obesity and overeating for example. Since people with binge eating disorder often suffer from muscle pain due to obesity, ginger is an excellent herb to help with lessening the pain. An additional perk is that it can also help with osteoarthritis.

3) Recognize Hunger and Satiety

Learning how to recognize hunger and satiety is one of the most important tasks when you start dealing with binge eating. The first lesson you should learn is that whenever you feel hunger, don't try to suppress it. On the contrary, address that feeling. Nevertheless, the way you are addressing it is what matters. So instead of staying hungry, use a snack, or have a cup of tea or water. We have already discussed many alternatives that you can use to deal with hunger at this point. The reason why we keep mentioning different types of food, variety, and frequency of meals is that hunger shouldn't be ignored. It is simple- if you ignore your need for food now, you will overeat later. Binge episodes are likely to happen if you push yourself toward avoiding food constantly. The mind wants to compensate for the hunger it felt before, so choosing not to is usually the wrong choice.

This is one of the tips on how you can learn to recognize cues that your mind and your body give you when it comes to satiety and hunger.

There are a few more ways that you can learn how to recognize and how to deal with both of these feelings. For example, try taking breaks between bites. That way you will slow down your eating and you will eat less food and get full at the same time. Additionally, you will enjoy your meal more. There is a saying that any meal should take at least 20 minutes to eat. Although sometimes it is not possible to have that amount of time for food, it is important to know that 20 minutes is more or less the amount of time that your body needs to balance stomach and hormones with the food intake and send your brain the information that it doesn't need more food. If you eat fast (all binge-eaters do), there is not enough time to process this information and you end up eating a lot more than you really need.

Again, you need to address your hunger, but you also need to learn how to recognize when you are feeling full without overeating. This leads us to another tip, and it is to avoid eating a second portion or a second plate. Of course, if you are feeling really hungry after these 20 minutes, you should eat until you are full. However, if that is not the case, getting seconds is actually overeating.

The temptation of eating something for a binge eater is strong as long as they can see the food. So one of the mechanisms you can use to avoid overeating is to remove everything edible from your sight. That will make temptation easier to overcome and once you eat your meal, the feeling of being full will be enough. Keep in mind that removing food from sight is not the same thing as restriction of food. If you are hungry, don't hide food from yourself because, as we already explained, the effect is contra-productive. However, removing food once you have had your normal meal is supposed to help you avoid eating unhealthy food that can be tempting in your surroundings during the day (the office for example).

These are all things that you can use to start learning how to listen to your body. Although binge eating can be challenging, our bodies are always trying to tell us what they need, and there is a difference between being physically hungry and having emotional overeating. Still, many still can't recognize the difference, which is why they try to fight BED with restrictive dieting that usually ends up with failure.

4) Look For Physical Activity You Like

When dealing with binge eating problems, the real goal is to replace bad habits with good ones and keep them for a long time. That is why it is also important to enjoy physical activities. It will help you feel better about yourself, and they are good for your health. Still, before you start spending money on different programs, you should find activities that will fit your personality. Another important factor is the amount of time that you have. There is a large number of physical activities that you can choose from, so instead of naming them, it is better to give yourself a few checkpoints that can help you find the right one.

Firstly, you should ask yourself about the kind of person you are. For example, if you are not a type who likes action maybe some yoga classes might look interesting On the other hand, if you really want action, then you will enjoy more activities like climbing, or you can start taking boxing classes for example.

Another important thing that we already mentioned is the amount of time that you have for physical activities. If you work too much, or if you have a family agenda all the time, try figuring out when you are free. Being free in the evening or in the morning will also limit your activity choices, also you might be free only 2 days a week after work for example. If that is the case, maybe home work out sessions are the best choice, there are plenty of combinations that you can find so you just decide the ones you like the most.

The third thing that you should have clear is the goal you want to achieve with that physical activity. For the beginning, long walks or swimming are maybe the best options for binge eaters or Pilates for relaxation. Another choice could be dancing, as it is fun and it is an excellent exercise.

Exercising alone or in a group is also one of the things that are important to determine the physical activity you will stick to. If you are not into socializing while exercising, you should avoid group activities such as dance and maybe take swimming lessons instead.

Whatever you find convenient, the goal is to be within

your budget too. If you like swimming but classes are too expensive, you have to find an alternative. For example, yoga is less expensive than climbing, but for walking you don't have to pay at all. Remember that being in shape doesn't matter, what matters is that you start with something enjoyable, and keep being persistent. A small success can be a great motivation. Small and easy steps and at one point, being physically active, is going to be a daily routine!

5) Learn to Recognize the Food that Really Satisfies You

As we already mentioned, the body always knows what it needs and if you learn how to listen, you will know how to make a difference between the essential need for food and your binge eating episodes. The real challenge and the right thing to do is to stop dieting and turn to a healthier way to deal with the eating problem. You will manage that if you tune your brain into recognizing the cues that your body gives you and then provide healthy answers to those cues. It is called intuitive eating. So the main difference between binge eating and intuitive eating is that you need intuitive eating to survive and make your body functional, while binge eating causes many unhealthy behaviors and consequences.

The only way you will learn how to recognize the food that satisfies you is to think about the reason for the craving. For example, if you crave something sweet, is the reason for that stress some other negative emotion, or is it because you feel like your blood sugar is low and that something sweet will raise your energy levels? Or if you are feeling sad, maybe having your favorite piece of cake will really make you feel better.

The difference here is that when you have a binge eating episode, you always feel guilty, but if you really enjoy the food and it changes everything. Every time you crave to eat something, keep in mind that there has to be a reason for it. Whether you are going to enjoy your food or not, depends on that reason. In both cases, craving has to be satisfied, but if you determine that specific food will make you happy rather than miserable and guilty, you should just enjoy it.

6) Eat With Taste. Give Yourself Something Good and Sweet

When you are a binge eater, or when you are dealing with weight in general, everyone keeps telling you that you have to avoid indulgent foods. So every time a binge eater has an episode and eats something sweet, the feeling of guilt is immense. This contra-productive technique is not something you should concern yourself with. Many types of research show that even biologically, we need sweets. So it is not something that you should feel guilty about.

Still, that doesn't mean that you should eat sweets all the time. In both cases, treats are something that you should allow yourself every now and then. Treats are embodied in our culture and socialization process, so you have a birthday cake or dessert after lunch. Struggling with binge eating doesn't mean that you should just cut out all sweets. Also, it doesn't mean that you need to feel guilty every time you look at the piece of cake. Enjoying food is good and it actually helps to deal with eating disorders. As you know, the main reason for binge eating is actually some negative emotion, so learning how to make a difference between intuitional eating and binge eating and learning how to enjoy the food you need for actual satisfaction of your hunger needs is more than you can achieve than with any diet. It is good for your health too.

Treating yourself to something sweet is a diversity that you should be joyful about. That way you will have a good motivation to keep up maintaining all other healthy choices that you need to help you deal with BED.

7) The Diet/Binge Circle

We have mentioned this several times, but it is one of the most important things that need to be understood. Binge eating episodes start as a result of deprivation that we impose on our bodies, it is not that we became insatiably hungry or too greedy. It is really simple, the more restrictions we put on our food choices, the more we will want to eat.

Rebellion is a term that we are all familiar with. When you deny your body something, it will rebel, it is really that simple. The more you resist the cues that the body gives you, the more you will feel the need to eat the food that is "forbidden". When you push something forcefully, most likely it will push back, at least that is what it is called a "law of nature". The reason it is hard to escape the circle of dieting and binge eating is that when you are dieting, you are suppressing your appetite all the time. Basically, this means that you are suppressing some basic instincts along the way, which is why we were talking about making a difference between real hunger and binge eating. The suppressed appetite can't go away, it can only build-up to the point where you have to satisfy it. But the worst part is that since you are restricting yourself from certain food, it becomes easy to lose control, and you end up overeating. This need for satisfying hunger after the length restriction is very intensive so in most cases, binging is the outcome.

Generally speaking, the diet-binge circle is a body reaction because it doesn't feel free to consume the nutrients it needs. The body knows from its instincts that the diet will continue immediately so it uses that "chance" of eating as much as it can and you end up having a binge episode where you can sometimes even be uncomfortable from the amount of food you have taken. Under the given circumstances, the body responds to all inputs, and if you suppress it too much, its natural answer will just extend the circle of dieting and binging.

8) The Hunger/Food Connection

Chronic disease and feelings of insecurity about food often begin when a family or a person (someone living alone) doesn't have enough money to afford healthy food, which means that from the beginning there are people who live under these poor conditions when it comes to nutrients and stress. These conditions are often premises for developing all kinds of chronic diseases, and BED among them. Additionally, once the BED appears, many people don't have enough money to address these issues, so it is hard to get adequate therapy, medication, and overall healthy food. This is the cycle that continues so whenever there is hunger, the real advancement in dealing with BED depends on the food that you can choose to eat to satisfy that hunger. Maintaining good health can be extremely difficult if there is a combination of poor conditions and poor knowledge.

9) Stop Dieting and Other Bad Habits /Create Sustainable Eating and Living Habits

If you choose to make a radical change, it won't do any good. As you can see, if you don't change your habits, eating just a veggie soup all day long won't do anything in the long run. Dieting can help losing weight but it won't help. So you should just quit the idea of restricting everything and try creating healthier habits instead. It will take time to permanently improve your habits in all aspects, but you can use the tips we mentioned above and start slowly. There is one efficient approach you should consider combining with all the advice we will mention in this book and it is divided into three simple steps:

To reflect on the way you were eating until now, to try to recognize and list all your eating habits and determine the ones that have the worst effect on your body. Also, try to determine all the triggers that cause your unhealthy behavior.

The next step is to replace habits that you determined to be bad. A lot of healthy habits were given in the sections above.

The last step is to reinforce these new habits.

It takes time and patience to change a habit, especially when dealing with a lot of emotional changes in the meantime. However, it is not impossible so as long as you have the will, you can make it.

Chapter 4

The Mindfulness-Based Eating Solutions

Mindful eating is being aware that nourishes your body and your spirit and opens the door to enjoy and welcome life. Let's think about our food for a minute... What did you have for your last meal? Go through each ingredient but don't do the calorie count. Just take a moment to appreciate the fact that and take appreciation of the path each ingredient had to go on until it got on your plate. Take everything into consideration, seasoning, and preparation of the food. There is a lot more to a meal than meets the eye.

Focus on one of the ingredients and notice what it took for it to get on your table. All the work and effort farmers took to grow that particular food. Think about the Sun, the soil, rain, growth, transportation, storage and all the other little things required for the food to grow. When you start thinking about what it takes to grow food, you become more thankful and acknowledge the true worth of an ingredient.

Mindful eating is all about having a healthy relationship with your food, rather than just inhaling it. It is undeniably not about dieting, but it does help you eat less.

Sit down when you eat; it is a lot harder being mindful of your food while you are standing up. Always use a plate and serve yourself a portion of food, rather than just eating from the pot or carton. Just focus on eating, don't work, talk or read while you eat. Spend some time chewing the food; savor each flavor you feel on your tongue. Drink enough water, but don't drink it during meals or right after; it is preferable to drink water at least 30 minutes before you eat. Planning your meals ahead of time helps you reduce mindless grabbing from the snack cabinet.

Mindfulness

Mindfulness is simply being aware of the happenings that take place right now and not wishing it all was different. It is just enjoying the pleasant without clinging to it when it changes, and it will change. It is enduring the unpleasant without fear that it wouldn't change because it will.

Remember, you create your own calm and that enables you to be here now, to be present. Focus yourself on the present moment calmly acknowledge and accept your feelings, sensations, and thoughts. Don't let yourself entangled with the past or the future, anger, worry or anxiety. Pull yourself to the now and feel life and its impact.

Mindfulness can be cultivated through practice, such as meditation, so try it out. Being mindful benefits us in so many different ways that include sleeping better, improved immune system, greater focus and concentration, increased empathy, compassion, happiness and optimism, and reducing stress and anxiety.

Intuitive Eating

Intuitive eating is an approach to health that has nothing to do with diets and it helps you get in touch with your own body, its signals, it breaks the dieting that goes on and off and heals your relationship with food.

Humans are born as natural intuitive eaters, but as we grow older restrictions and rules are set around food, we lose this ability. With intuitive eating there is no counting calories or food restrictions, you can eat everything. This is not a diet, it is more of a lesson we want our body to learn. It is a re-learning process, where you put your focus on signals that come from the body. Permit yourself to have what your body wants. Don't make a difference between "good food" and "bad food". Now you can eat all kinds of foods with no regret. You can have it. But, one other thing usually happens and it is called reverse psychology. Now that you can have it, it appears that you don't really want it.

Mindless Eating

Mindless eating comes when you are not focused or aware of the quantity of the food you intake or that you are eating in the first place. It often takes place with some other activity simultaneously going on. For example, watching TV and eating chips out of the bag and before you know it, there are no more chips. Or, you are sitting at work at your office desk while the bowl of chocolates next to you slowly depletes to three. Or even maybe you feel guilty about wasting food, so you eat everything on your plate, even though you realized you were full a few moments ago.

Mindless eating can impact weight loss goals as it contributes to your calorie intake. These kinds of habits can happen to all of us, and it probably did at one point. Because we get busy and stressed, we start multitasking. We reach for food without really thinking about hunger, eat without really enjoying the fullness of taste and getting a meal just becomes almost like a chore.

Beginning steps to take:

It is important to identify behaviors that lead to mindless eating. When you find yourself in that autopilot eating mode, become aware of this habit, and try to notice what you are doing while you undertake mindless eating. These actions are usually something like watching TV, working on a project on a laptop, driving in the car, etc.; but it is important to think about what else you could replace food within these scenarios. For example, try crocheting or knitting in front of the TV, replace food with a warm cup of tea, listen to some podcasts while driving.

We already talked about the weekly meal plan. Work out what you are going to make during the week, make a shopping list and shop for the ingredients. This will help you stay organized and focused, it will save your budget as you won't buy any unnecessary food.

Incorporate movements into your daily life, we all know exercise is one of the crucial health components. Find time for some short walk or gentle stretching in the evening. Create mindful eating affirmations, because they will help you in two ways. As for the first reason, with affirmations, you have a constant reminder of what is important to you, and secondly, because they work to rewire your brain in a way that affirmation becomes second nature to you.

Get Off the Diet

Yes, we all want to lose that weight and we all think diets are the quickest way to achieve it. But the real goal is not losing weight in a short period and getting it back again. The goal is being in control. You have to learn how to be in control of your eating and the answer here is to stop trying to be in control. Whenever we put restrictions on our food, for example, you forbid yourself from sweets; it will just create a bigger craving for that food. So get off the diets and start seeing and making a mental notice of the quantity of food you eat daily. Deprivation doesn't work and it doesn't do any good for your physical and mental health.

Dieting is stressful to the body. You are suddenly cutting it off of some ingredients and therefore messing with metabolic and biochemical reactions occurring in the body. Diets make you ignore all the signals your body is sending.

Set One Goal (Besides Weight Loss) To Get You

Started

Setting goals beyond weight loss is essential if you want to stick with a weight-loss program. And setting goals that don't have a direct connection to the weight loss can help you reach your goal weight sooner. You don't have to be always focused on fitting on the scale. It is important to find a way that works in the long run.

You could focus on getting stronger or faster, which will help you build your muscles and speed up your metabolism, which are the things that lead to weight loss. Or maybe you could set a goal like fast-walking with a friend or alone for several days a week or just taking your dog out hiking every weekend. But one of the most important goals is health. Reduce your blood pressure, decrease the usage of medications, improve your cholesterol levels, etc.

Mindfulness Definition: (Intention, Attention, Attitude)

We have already talked about mindfulness. Maybe you have already tried practicing it. Maybe you think mindfulness is just meditating, but that wouldn't be the case.

Let's take a look at mindfulness definition according to the American Psychological Association (APA.org, 2012):

"...a moment-to-moment awareness of one's

experience without judgment. In this sense, mindfulness is a state and not a trait. While it might be promoted by certain practices or activities, such as meditation, it is not equivalent to or synonymous with them."

As we can see, mindfulness is not static nor are some people just born more mindful than the others. It is the basic ability to be present and observe without criticism that all humans have.

In short, mindfulness is intentionally paying attention. Setting an intention is like setting a direction in which you want to go. It represents creating a commitment to carrying out any action you want to. Intention consists of planning and forethought. Intentions are not goals. They are more about what kind of person you want to be, how you wish to contribute to the outer world, and how you choose to involve yourself with the lives of other people.

Another term associated with mindfulness is attention. Attention is a multidimensional cognitive process that includes the ability to focus on the important and it is the ability to persistently mentally engage while performing tasks that require a lot of mental energy. Attention training is an important aspect of being mindful.

Awareness is our ability to feel our conscious side of the mind. We could explain consciousness as a clear blue sky and the mind exist within that consciousness just like clouds in the sky. The sky doesn't criticize the clouds, it accepts them; they are just there. Sometimes the clouds enclose the sky, but we are always aware that the sky is still there. Just like these clouds, our thoughts sometimes overshadow our minds, but our consciousness is always there behind all that noise. Then, awareness is our ability to see that there are clouds in the sky; it is our attention focused and directed to a more specific aspec

Mindful Eating

As we said before, mindful eating is a technique that helps you gain more control over your eating habits. Use mindfulness to reach that state where you pay attention to your physical cues about eating.

Eating mindfully is, first of all being aware of hunger. Are you really hungry? Appreciate the food and make yourself comfortable while you eat. That means no eating out of the bags or containers, plate everything. And when we are at it, create a beautiful table too. Put pretty dishes, napkins, and flowers. And savor and enjoy every bite. When you are eating slower, you will notice that you are eating less. It takes about 20 minutes for a signal from your stomach to reach your brain about you being full.

Be mindful of what you are eating, because sugar, salt and other chemicals in highly processed food create the same chemical reaction that makes drug addicts crave cocaine. Before eating ask yourself why, what, when, how, how much and where. Answering these questions can keep you eating healthier and even decide if you are really hungry.

Breath and Belly Check for Hunger and Satiety before You Eat

Relax your body and take a deep breath. Connect with the sensations of your body. Do you feel any sensations of physical hunger? How hungry are you on a scale of 1-10? What are you hungry for? You might be thirsty, as the center for hunger and center for thirst are located near each other in our brains. But, then again, you might be hungry for something entirely different from food. Pick up what your body is telling you. Breathing here has a huge role, as if you have shallow breath, you might feel more stressed than the next person. Then again, shallow breathing leads to more anxiety and stress, which leads to our unconscious decisions about food, for example, overeating. Why? Because food reduces stress, but then you find yourself eating whenever you are stressed, and when you eat under stress, your body is more prone to store food as fat. It creates a loop. As you breathe in more oxygen, you get yourself in a relaxed state and your body can metabolize food more successfully.

So, you can see some stress symptoms cause that feeling of hunger, but not every uncomfortable feeling you have is hunger. Eventually, with mindful eating, you will start to notice the difference.

It may take some time, but checking in with your

belly can become your ally in mindful eating. The first step to eat normally is to honor your physical hunger, don't live to eat, but eat to live.

Assess Your Food

Observe your food, see what it looks like, and notice those colors and smells. Recognize it and think about where it came from. You don't need a lot of time to do this, but it can give you a lot of information about what you are about to eat. As you take your first bite, chew it thoroughly and feel the taste. Reexamine if that is what you wanted to eat. Don't just throw food in your mouth before assessing what it really is. It happens easily, mindless eating kicks in, and before you know it, you are eating something just because it is in front of you.

You can even get a sense about how healthy is this food just by the way it smells, looks or feels. Sense does your body want it or not. You can even practice by holding different kinds of food into our hands, feeling the texture and the shape, smelling it and tuning with your body to sense the reaction to certain foods.

But if you are more prone to eating processed food, it will be difficult to use your senses to guide you. Primitive reward centers in the brain are triggered by foods that have a high sugar value, salt or fat and give out the same responses found in drug addicts.

As you start practicing assessing your food, notice if your body desires a particular food for its taste; if so, you have developed a biological craving for that particular food. Assessing your food is not about counting calories, fats or carbohydrates. We have learned to choose our food by the numbers, not by the nutritional value or health impact it has on our body. Something can have a low-calorie value, and not do your body good, because it probably has some other substances that are not good for your health. Don't block out your natural body wisdom; your body knows what it needs.

With learning how to assess your food, you will learn that healthier and natural choices are more in line with what your body wants and needs. As you start observing the food you eat daily, you will become more sensitive to the cravings of the body, not the mind. Your mindful attention is going to lead you with the taste and smell of the food to keep eating that type of food.

Investigate Your Hunger throughout the Meal

As mentioned earlier, it takes 20 minutes for a signal about satiety from the stomach to get to the brain. So it is really important to examine your hunger and satiety throughout the meal. If you bring the hunger to your attention in the middle of the meal, you might find that you are not hungry anymore; even if there is still food on your plate.

We have learned to clean our plates, not to waste

food. But it is okay even if you don't eat everything, you have eaten the amount your body needed. Give yourself permission to stop.

Don't rush through the meal, start embracing the idea that you will stop halfway through it and maybe not continue with eating.

Pay attention to your belly and if you are satisfied and not hungry anymore, stop eating. But if you are still hungry, continue eating while, but still, keep in mind mindful eating.

Stopping at eating at the point of being satisfied is not so easy, just because we don't feel full. But that is one of the greatest challenges to overcome. But keep in mind this, if you eat to the point of fullness, you will feel drowsy and heavy and in the other case, you are good to go. Sometimes we keep eating just because food is very tasty; it is appealing to our taste buds. If this is the situation, it is good to remind yourself that this is not the only time you can have food as tasty as that. And you can always pack it up for later or just throw it away.

Chew Your Food Thoroughly and Slowly

As you chew your food, pay attention to the sensations that food produced in your mouth. Detect all the different tastes and whether you enjoy them. Notices how long does it take for you to chew the food before you swallow it. Chew each bite thoroughly.

Mindful eating brings your attention to taking its sweet time to savor your food. You need to slow down while eating and you do that by bringing your attention to chewing and feeling the taste as you chew. Chewing is important both biologically and mindfully. In terms of biology, chewing food sends signals for processing. It breaks down our food into small pieces, triggers the enzymes, and saliva starts flowing in. Within the saliva, there is an enzyme called amylase, which breaks down complex sugars. Enzymes break food down even further so it can be digested absorbed by the digestive system.

The sense of taste is activated when you put the food is in your mouth. It is the signal that helps your body to identify compounds, determine if they are good or bad, and then processes them accordingly. When you chew mindfully, you send a message to your brain and it accelerates the production of saliva, which is good for teeth health.

Mindful chewing enables you to slow down and enjoy the taste of your food, which is really important if we want to practice mindful eating.

Savor Your Food

Savoring your food means fully appreciating and enjoying it completely. It means tasting it comprehensively. When you taste something, you are actually tasting the chemical composition of the food. Choose the food that you really like. It is important that you always try to honor your taste buds along with your body. Savoring the food means that you are completely present for the experience of eating. It means that you put your body and your soul into id, and into pleasure that it provides. Drive your attention to the range of those sensations in your mouth, available as you chew. If you can't enjoy your food, why would you choose to eat it in the first place?

Take your time consciously choosing the food you are going to eat. If you have a desire for a certain ingredient, let yourself mindfully enjoy it. Don't go on eating all sorts of different kinds of food and in the end giving in and eat what you craved in the first place. For example, if you want to eat chocolate, no matter how many apples you eat, you'll still be craving chocolate.

Through the studies, it is shown that the sense of taste is something that we acquire. According to researches, if you expose yourself to certain foods for a certain period, you will start preferring them. However, it is possible to train taste buds through mindful eating. But, you don't have to force yourself. Yes, you can mindfully eat fast food, but have it and savor it, enjoying each bite. Just really pay attention to how the food tastes. At least three times a day you have a chance to have a pleasant experience with food. Just do not stop paying attention.

Facing Your Forbidden Food

It is important to confront our fears in every aspect in life and especially with food. We label some types of food as "bad" and the other as "good", but what are we really doing? We are blaming the food rather than on ourselves and our control in enjoying these kinds of foods. Write down what scares you about your forbidden food. It might be something like fear of your sweet tooth and not being able to stop once you indulge yourself. You are afraid you will get fat and your significant other will leave you. It is okay. Write it down. When it is on paper it is easier to decide if it is as scary as you think.

Remember, it is not the food you fear; only the potential effect it might have on you.

Familiarize yourself with your off-limits foods. Chew it slowly and really feel the taste. You will start noticing that these kinds of foods are not really scary. Maybe the reason you crave them is that you learned they were bad for you and even because you keep them in that forbidden file in your head.

Come up with positive instead of a negative. Instead of saying you hate one type of food, say how you enjoy the other; instead of rejecting what you don't want, you are choosing the thing you want.

Banish the forbidden food concept from your mindset. It is really not necessary to give up on food unless you are a diabetic or you have allergies. When you forbid yourself of certain foods, you only crave them more. And trust yourself.

Usually, when we fear food it is not the food we are afraid of. We are afraid of ourselves and not being in control. But when you remove that label you put on, the appeal disappears. Let your forbidden food become just another food.

Eating With Permission

Permission to eat, in the beginning, might look like eating more foods we kept our distance from for so long. And usually, that is any kind of food that the diet world demonizes. But it is true though; a lot of those foods aren't as nutritionally valuable as other, healthier options. So, when giving ourselves permission to eat, we must also take nourishment and satisfaction into consideration.

Even by just telling yourself that you are allowed to eat any food that you want and that nothing is off-limits, the intense desire to eat those kinds of foods decline. It all comes down to allowing yourself to experience these foods and that is the way the food becomes less of a novelty since we start realizing that we can have it whenever we want to.

You don't need to fear overindulgence in these kinds of foods, because there is something known as habituation response. This process explains that we quickly adapt to repeated stimuli, and with every repetition, we derive less pleasure from it. When we are dieting or keeping food restrictions we don't practice habituation. It doesn't allow you to get that repeated exposure often enough so that the food doesn't seem so appealing anymore.

Eating the Right Amount

If we are not in tune with our body, we might ask ourselves "How much should I eat?" But the truth is that it differs from person to person. It depends on your age, weight, metabolism, sex, how active you are, and many other factors. For example, a very physically active person might eat more calories than a person who goes for a walk every now and then.

Again, it all comes down to listening to the cues your body provides you with. Don't overindulge in any kinds of food, because too much of anything is poisonous. It might be bad for your body, or your brain, memory or overall health.

Knowing and Respecting Your Habits and Triggers with Food

As you start this journey, you discover a lot of things about your body and feelings. Get to know your habits and emotional triggers when it comes to food, it will help you in this battle in the long run. Knowing your strengths as well as weaknesses can be a determinant of your success.

Build habits around food and respect the time you invested in discovering what works for you. We are all different, but we all deserve the best we can be.

Chapter 5

What Are You Really, Really Hungry For?

It makes you think. The question "What am I really hungry for?" opens up many possible answers as it opens further questions. Am I fulfilled? Am I happy? Do I crave for love? Or comfort? Am I just bored?

Life is about being happy and fulfilled; one doesn't go without the other. Most of us lead stressful, complicated lives, and that is the reality. Don't we lose ourselves in the rush of every day? We find ourselves in that state most of the time. But the most important thing we are losing is self-awareness, and you know what is funny? We are not aware of it! We just wake up one day, look in the mirror and don't have any recognition of the person in the mirror.

And, if your life isn't fulfilled, no amount of food can compensate for that. Food is a quick fix that doesn't solve anything. Yes, you can say that your life is way too overbearing and that you can't find time to deal with these kinds of things, and when you say that it sounds like an excuse that stops you from being the best version of yourself. You say it because of the stress, anxiety, fear of failure and not believing in yourself and you become your saboteur.

Your best intentions to change your life go to waste, just because you don't believe the change is possible. Bad memories and bad habits cling to you as much as you cling to them. And just because those are familiar, you find that it has to be what you deserve. But you still have a deep desire for happiness and that right there is your best motivation.

So, are you fulfilled? Are you happy? What are you hungry for?

Emotional Eating

Do you find yourself rushing to find something in the fridge when you are feeling upset or down? Finding food comforting is very common, and it is a part of emotional eating. Emotional eating is an issue that affects both sexes and we find the root cause of this in everyday struggles. People who emotionally eat reach for food to make themselves feel better, to soothe the negative feelings or suppress them. And after this, they might even feel guilt or shame, which leads to more emotional eating.

Now, humans have to eat in order to survive, so it is really difficult to distinguish between real hunger and emotional hunger. Let's talk about that for a bit. Real or physical hunger is built slowly over time and it makes you crave a variety of food groups. And when you have enough food your stomach sends a signal to the brain that you are full. Physical hunger isn't connected to negative feelings about eating.

Emotional hunger comes suddenly and abruptly, and you want to satisfy it immediately. You crave only certain foods, which are usually high in sugar or carbohydrates. You may binge on food and not feel any sensation of fullness, and that could make you feel guilty or ashamed about eating in the first place.

How do we overcome this? The first and most important step is in finding a different, healthier outlet for your negative emotions. Grab a book, listen to music, write a journal, and go for a walk or a jog. Engage our mind in some different activities that relieve stress, so you don't reach for food comfort.

Food Like: Entertainment and Freedom from Boredom, Comfort and Escape, Love

Wait, how did you end up opening the fridge door? What is it? Oh, cake leftovers...

Eating out of boredom is pointless. When we are bored, what we look at in food is entertainment. How does the food entertain us, you may ask? Tasty and sugar foods release hormones of happiness, which are highly addictive. It is almost taking a hit of cocaine and feeling euphoric, or falling head over heels and wanting our object of affection near us. Whatever our obsession is, dopamine and serotonin make us want more of it. Sometimes, when you are bored, you might just want a bag of chips, just to feel that crunching and hear that sound. Again, we are usually not aware of this, but we know we want it now.

We also find comfort in food, for the same reasons, happy hormones are released in our brain. It is a quick fix for emotions we can't deal with right now. We see people comforting themselves with food everywhere; in movies, commercials, at home when mom had a stressful day at work and she grabs that can of ice-cream. But it is a highly addictive game we play with ourselves and again we are not aware of this.

So, the key to solving this definitely would be love, but what kind of love? The answer is simple. It is self-love. Self-love leads you into self-awareness, which is the key component to succeed in anything. This doesn't mean that you have to be self-judgmental actually; it is seeing and discovering who you are so you can grow.

Understanding and Accepting Unpleasant Emotions

As we have begun exploring ourselves, it is important to realize that negative emotions are completely normal. We all feel them, but the difference is how we respond to them. Some of us tend to vocalize them, some might have a violent reaction, and others just hide them or suffocate them with food, drugs or alcohol.

Start paying attention to what might be the trigger or the cause of your negative emotions. In terms of causes, negative emotions could be such as anxiety because of a project at school or work; sadness because of a break-up; despair for not being able to stick to that new diet; anger because you have been stuck on one assignment for hours and similar. But, we don't want to cut the negative emotions out of our life; happiness isn't the absence of these emotions, because no emotion is without purpose. Unpleasant emotions are normal, helpful and healthy parts of our life. You need to learn new ways to respond to these emotions in a way that helps you grow and for your general well-being. In your lifetime you will feel a wide range of emotions with different intensity.

Managing Your Emotions

Having the power and control over your emotions at any given moment is one of the greatest skill sets one can obtain. Learning how to manage your emotions is essential if you want to live a life you own and direct completely. It is important to take notice that every emotion you feel, you are not feeling it because you have to. You are feeling it because you chose to. Yes, you can choose how you want to feel at any given moment. You can decide that you feel good, right now at this very moment.

The first step to mastering your emotions is being able to identify them. You can start by asking yourself questions like what are you feeling at the moment, or are you sure that you are feeling that exactly and not something else. Analyze your emotion, get curious. Emotions are felt for certain reasons and can teach you valuable lessons about yourself, such as how to overcome emotional blocks.

Get confident that you can control your emotions. To learn how to control your emotions, you need to consciously choose the emotional responses you experience. The next step is learning how to detach yourself from emotional triggers. Emotional triggers could be people around you, places or things that trigger certain feelings. Learn how to forgive yourself and others or things that triggered your emotions and it'll prove to be a key in detaching yourself from the problems that accompany them. Learn how to allow people to be people.

Try to see the bigger picture of everything in your life, and even in a storm of emotionally upsetting moments, trust that it serves a greater purpose. All in all, how you respond to situations in life is what makes the difference. No matter how tough it may seem, you can always choose to feel differently and control your emotional state.

Mindfulness of Emotions

First of all, you aren't at mercy of your emotions, your brain creates them. It is important to understand where the emotion came. Whatever you might be feeling now is directly connected with how you move your body. If you keep your head and shoulders down, it could lead to feeling depressed, so to feel better, straighten your spine and chin up!

Also, language can deeply influence our emotional state, especially your inner monologue. If you keep on thinking, "Why do these things always happen to me?" it will create a negative state of mind, but if you were to ask yourself something like, "How can I turn this to my advantage? How can I benefit from this?" you are creating a positive mindset. If you are feeling negative about something, take a closer look at your thoughts and words.

On the other hand, it is really important to focus on the good. Ask yourself where you want to go, what you want to accomplish, rather than keeping that mindset of uncertainty. Influence your emotions by thinking about how can you move and act toward a more positive outcome. You'll be able to make tough decisions, unlock your potential and enjoy life at any given moment. We should be mindful of our emotions because blindly following our emotions can lead us to decisions we might regret.

Broadening the Focus

To get fulfillment in this life we need to be self-aware, but also we need to strive to become the best we can be. We do that by learning new skills, you might fall in love, for example crocheting or learning the languages. Broadening our knowledge broadens our view of the world, of the important and valuable things in our life. Learning new skills also takes away boredom, makes us feel more accomplished and thus, happier. The more you see, the more you understand. The more you learn about the world around you, the more you learn about yourself.

Learning the Lesson

The universe doesn't let you get away with anything. Neither does your body; your body is a personal record of everything you've done in your life. Is your fight with weight a lesson that keeps repeating for you? We have the ability to recognize that life provides us with countless opportunities to heal and develop ourselves as stronger, and then we feel a sense of freedom. It is a cliché, but every day is a new opportunity to start overcoming your boundaries.

Honoring Your Immediate Needs

Your immediate needs are food, water, shelter, and clothes. You are not honoring your immediate needs by indulging in any of them. Honoring your needs means realizing that not everyone has the luxury of having a place to sleep or enough food for a week, and being grateful for what you have. Gratitude is one of the healthiest emotions a human can have. The more you are grateful for what you have, the bigger the chance that you will have more to be grateful for. Did you know that gratitude can improve self-esteem, relieve stress, improve sleep and relationships and rewire your brain?

Discovering Your Values and Dreams

Discover your values as your core beliefs and your guiding principles, because they shape your roles in daily life. These values direct your passions, interests, your thoughts, and words and act as a pointer towards your decisions. Determining our values helps you plan for your career and financial goals, how you spend your time, academic goals, etc. Values are those things you believe to be of essential importance in the way you live, function and interact with others. These values represent the measures by which you judge yourself and others. It is important to find core values because when some action is not aligned with your core values, you feel conflicted, so it is really important to determine whether our dream supports your core values or if it clashes with these.

As important as discovering your value is discovering your dream in life. What do you truly wish to accomplish? What makes your soul feel alive? What makes you feel that spark? These questions are not easy to answer, but you must reflect and be clear and decisive about what you want.

Emotionally Renewing Yourself

We have all been there: maybe you are exhausted from a long week at work, or maybe you are having relationship problems, or maybe you are just tired because of a long caring for your little kids. At moments like this, ordering a pizza, buying a box of chocolates and eating and watching Netflix until you fall asleep sounds like heaven. But that is never enough. What you need is something on a deeper level, a kind of refreshment. What you really need is emotional renewal.

Emotional renewal is restoring balance with our emotions so we can operate and stay on our path. You might think that emotional renewal requires going on a weekend-long spiritual trip in nature, even though that is a good idea it is not the only solution. Take a walk to the park, sit and enjoy the air and bird songs. Connect with nature; notice the trees, water, grass, wind, which allows you to bring your attention out of your mind, allowing you to relax. If you have access to the ocean, lake or river, spend some time just observing the waves or flow of the water, it is relaxing and renewing for a lot of people. And if you don't have this option available, you can listen to wave sounds on your computer.

This goes under the self-care. Take time to replenish your soul.

Food Strategy

It's known that the food we eat plays a major role in establishing our metabolism, self-esteem, hormonal regulations and overall vitality. Food has energetic characteristics that affect our health, moods, and emotions. People often eat a lot of wrong foods. Most frequently they eat fast food, and they don't feel remorse. But when they start dieting, especially if they do it sporadically, they create a yo-yo effect without cultivating healthy habits that can actually contribute to their health and longevity. With our food strategy, we need to bring back the balance in our organism.

One of the strategies that you can use is to start a daily journal and write down the food you eat. This is a useful technique because most of us just eat mindlessly. We don't spend time thinking about the nutrition value of certain foods. When you start keeping a journal about food, you start taking more care of food choices. Once you start doing this, you can start changing and eliminating bad eating habits that make you gain weight. More importantly, you can change bad habits that influence your immunity and overall health.

The other method is to remove unhealthy food from your fridge and pantry. Making this cleanout work you will stop yourself from eating whatever is available. You should clean out everything, from candies to canned goods with sodium, Make sure, you replace those items with a lot of vegetables and fruits.

I recommend emphasizing plant-based protein nutrition. Plant-based proteins evoke anti-inflammatory and alkaline ash supporting the body's immune processes and self-repair. Plants rich in proteins to add to your diet are lentils, almonds, peas, beans, oats, and quinoa.

Next, incorporate foods that have medicinal effect or foods that have immune-boosting effects. Some options include Brussels sprouts, cabbage, kale, broccoli, etc. Also, integrate a lot of colors in our diet, for every meal try to eat at least three vegetables of a different color.

There is a large number of food strategies that you can use for creating better eating habits and for improving your mind and your looks at the same time. You can even mix two or more food strategies to create something that will fit your needs. If doing so, you will increase your mental and physical vitality, and you will feel much better about yourself.

List of Foods To Eat and Avoid. Just Kidding, Let's Do Something Smarter

This will sound funny, but it is the best advice. Eat only when you are hungry. Seriously, ask yourself are you that hungry, are you eating out of boredom or are you just feeling a bit down? Whichever it is, deal with it, and don't suffocate yourself with food.

I am not going to give you a list of which foods you should eat and which you should avoid. We have already covered that. Let's talk about the time when we eat the most. It is usually at night when we have finished the work for the day or sent the kids to bed, you sit on the sofa just to watch a TV show, but suddenly you need something to nibble on while you watch the show. Instead of reaching for food, consider making yourself a nice and warm cup of tea or maybe some cocoa if you are not a tea fan. This way, the hot beverage will warm you up and fulfill the hunger.

Try not to eat past 7 pm; it is ancient wisdom that dinner shouldn't be a huge meal. Avoid refined sugars as much as possible, not drinking soft drinks will have a great impact on you losing weight over the year course. Accept that changes are processes that need time. You will thank yourself, three months from now.

Moving in Ways That Feel Delicious

Never forget, your ability to move is a gift, so respect, love and take care of your body. Stop for a second and realize how fortunate you are to be able to just get up and go where you want to go. The only way you can feel truly alive is by moving your body, by feeling our body and becoming conscious of what it is able to do.

Exercise. Not too many people like hearing this word. Why? Because those few times they tried exercising, they felt like they were run over by a bus. Well, guess what, every beginning feels like that like you just can't do it. But you need dedication and consistency, you need to win a fight against yourself, and that is the most difficult battle to win.

Just start today, because no matter how slow you go, you are beating everyone that still clings to the couch. Stay dedicated, love yourself enough to exercise and keep in mind that a little progress every day adds up to big results.

Exercise not only improves our posture or changes your body, but it also changes your attitude and your mind by releasing endorphins. This is the power of delicious moving. It becomes addictive.

What Exercise Does It For Me?

Losing weight is hard, but being overweight is also hard. You have to choose which hard you would rather deal with. A huge number of people that start with a losing weight plan, quit. But not you, not this time.

I wouldn't recommend just doing one type of workout and I don't recommend starting with an intense workout. You need to start adjusting our body to the movements, so I recommend starting with just a half-hour walk and later on, to an hour-long walk. Also, one of the great moderate-intensity exercises is bike riding, so give it a try. As you start feeling lighter on your feet, implement running for two minutes than walking for five minutes and so on. You will gain confidence that you can do this. And trust me, you can. After you began with moving your body, explore the different ways you could exercise and find the one, which suits you. But always change it up, just so you don't get bored and to challenge our body. For example, if you are going to the gym, do some yoga stretching exercises at home. It will help your muscles not ache as much.

Every Movement Counts

You don't have to break out sweat every day to reap the health benefits of being active. Any light physical activity can benefit your health goes. Light physical activity includes any behavior that isn't sitting down: walking to get mail, walking your dog and cleaning the shelves. Vacuuming the house is a great workout for your arms and your core. When you talk on your phone, walk around the room. Do errands clean behind the furniture, any housework goes, and the benefits are doubled. Every movement counts!

Make Your Workplace Active

If you are working in an office, you can find some workplace workouts online that you can do at your table, like some stretching and small exercises. Also, if you need something, don't wait for anyone to bring it to you, go and get it yourself, it is a great opportunity to take a walk and reset your brain.

The Benefit of Paying Attention

When you start paying attention to anything, you start noticing the ways you can improve it. When you start paying attention to your body, guess what? Yes. You start seeing all the things you could improve. For example, you start noticing your posture is bad, and once you start straightening up, you realize that those pesky headaches were because of that bad posture.

Moving Based On Your Age

At different ages, our body needs different types of exercises. During childhood, exercise helps healthy body development, controlling body weight, builds healthy bones and helps to create healthy sleep patterns. The recommendation for children is at least one hour of physical activity a day. Children should try different sports that help develop different sets of skills.

Exercise habits decline during the teenage years, especially in children that don't play competitive sports or children that are not so good at sports. Teens should be encouraged to get in on a team sport; it is beneficial for both physical and mental health.

In our 20s, we are at our absolute physical peak. Building bone density and lean muscle mass will be of great help with keeping in shape as you age.

In your 30s it is important to keep your cardiovascular fitness so you could slow down the physical decline of the body. Diversify your workout, try spin class and yoga.

Most people start putting on weight in their 40s, so you should take on running and some weight-training. Pilates is great to build core strength and prevent back pain.

In your 50 some chronic conditions may appear, there is a higher risk of heart conditions. Try something different, like tai-chi, which is excellent for relaxation and balance.

In our 60s and beyond, just try to be active as much as you can. Take on some dancing classes with our significant other or go for a gossip-filled walk with your lifelong friend.

Let's Get Started. Don't You Dare to Postpone!

Starting is difficult. Daring to start something and possibly fail is terrifying. But you know what is even more terrifying? Not trying again and again after we fail. We fail at difficult things, and we have to learn to overcome that difficulty. There is no room for negativity. If someone else can do it, so can you! Just start and keep pushing through. You know your strength; you know you can beat yourself, just so you can create a better you.

Make It Enjoyable

Incorporate some fun songs in your workout playlist, especially if those songs make you want to dance. And if you feel like dancing, dance, because as we said earlier, every move counts! This way you can make your workout fun. Or take up a dance class, maybe some Latino dances or hip-hop. That has to be a lot of fun.

Be Consistent

Exercising might feel like an unnecessary burden at first, but if you stay consistent, after some time exercising will feel like therapy. Being consistent is one of the keys to succeeding at anything. It is not about being perfect, it is about continuous effort and that is how transformation happens. Committing to a consistent training will build the body you want and strengthen your mind. Look ahead and prepare, don't look back and regret not starting today.

Schedule Activity in Your Day

Make a schedule or take a planner, and make plans week ahead. Remember to include some physical activity every single day, whether it is just a walk or full-on workout. Plan to do it, and commit to it. Don't change your plans for no one, respect your time. You are doing this for yourself and nobody else.

Visualize Yourself as an Acting Person

Visualization of our goals is important because it pushes us through difficult times or when we want to give up. Visualize yourself as that person that can do any of those workouts, and work until you get to that point.

Make Your Plan

Make your own workout plan; discover new exercises and new workout techniques. Find what works for you the best and implement it to your routine. Also, try and make a nutrition plan with the help of a trainer or a nutritionist and stick to it. Making a plan and going through with it is almost a guarantee that you will fulfill your goal.

LOVE YOURSELF.

Chapter 6

Making "Healthy Fast Food" In A Hurry-Up World

Even though in recent years there have been some menu additions, and some fast-food chains started offering healthier options, fast food is still one of the biggest nightmares when it comes to healthy eating, and fighting obesity in general. Although most people know that fast food has more negative than positive traits, statistics say that each day, approximately 9.5 million people in the USA eat some kind of fast food. On the other hand, unlike before, nowadays it is not impossible to find certain fast food options that can be seen as more healthy, so at least you won't have to worry about additional fat or cholesterol issues all the time.

The Perils of Convenience Eating

Although convenience food is easy to prepare and doesn't cost much money, it is not a food that is really convenient for health. Another name for convenience food is processed food. It is defined as a food that is prepared in large amounts (commercially) with the purpose of easy consumption. But eating convenience food doesn't provide any kind of nutrients that your body needs. On the contrary, instead of nutrients, processed food is full of sugar, sodium, and above all, saturated fats.

For people who have binge eating disorder, it is highly recommended to avoid this type of food, especially if they have any kind of heart disease. The same principle applies to those who have problems with diabetes. This is not a healthy food they should feed themselves with. Convenience food is often colored with chemicals that are obviously not organic and it is not uncommon that it has non-organic flavoring too. Furthermore, ingredients that can impact your health the most are preservatives such as MSG, and if someone who has binge episodes eats this kind of food regularly, it can feel consequences real fast. Obesity is increased in the shortest amount of time, and it is not uncommon that overweight comes with different kinds of diseases.

When it comes to the craving for this kind of food, it is more connected to the added flavors and unnatural textures that the real taste and use of food. The sensory overload of convenience food is achieved by using enormous amounts of fat and salt, and in no time a person becomes "addicted" to these products. For a binge eater, the need to satisfy taste can be a safe escape route when feeling stressed. Still, it is possible to avoid eating convenience food even if you have been eating it for a while. It will take some time to detox your body and your taste sensors and the best way to do that are to reduce convenience food gradually. As we explained in some of the previous chapters, making sudden changes can have the opposite effect. Since it is already far from natural, it is not surprising that processed food is often modified too. This means that it also takes time to digest it and that it doesn't have enough vitamins or minerals to keep a body healthy and functional. Some of the most popular convenience foods are packaged chips, salt, sugar, flour, bread, canned vegetables, frozen meals and pre-packaged foods, commercialized fruit juices, and by far the most popular convenience foods are fast food menu items.

Still, it is not like you don't have any alternatives. For example, instead of potato chips, you can make your own, homemade chips. Just buy some sweet potatoes and slice them into thin pieces. Use olive oil to fry them, and you have the same product, but much tastier and healthier than the one from the bag. Note that you should avoid ketchup and try using some organic dips instead.

Another alternative and we mentioned that several times already, is to use fresh fruits and veggies, there is no need to buy canned ones. Even if a can says that vegetables inside have a "low amount" of sodium, that is still much more sodium than in seasonal, fresh veggie brought from the grocery.

Also, instead of commercial orange juice, why not just drink fresh-squeezed orange juice instead? It is simple to do, and the health benefits of fresh juice are incomparable to the juice from the tetra pack. Freshly squeezed juices (from both fruits and vegetables) are very rich with nutrients. They can serve as an energy boost too.

It is no secret that more and more people tend to prepare pre-packed meals because they lack time to prepare something else. However, if you plan your time better, you can always spare some free time during the weekend and prepare food for a few days. It is not the same when you eat pre-packed food and homemade food that comes out of the fridge after a day or two. The second option is still healthier and more nutritious than the first will ever be.

Junk Food. Because We Like It and How to Do Without It

Junk food is not healthy, and it is something that more or less everybody knows. It has poor nutritional value and it can cause problems with blood pressure, cholesterol, and heart. There are even studies that connect junk food with depression. And if you go back to the causes of binge eating disorder, you will realize that junk food is one of the biggest challenges for a binge eater, especially during its overeating episodes. And even if it is common knowledge that junk food isn't good we still eat it all the time. According to some food specialists, there are two main reasons why junk food seems pleasurable, hence sometimes addictive.

The first reason is related to the fact that junk food provides a feeling of eating real food (taste is distinctive; it smells a certain way, and most of the time you have a feeling in your mouth that you want to last). The scientific term for this taste phenomenon is known as ''oro-sensation''. It is one of the main reasons why many companies spend large amounts of money to determine what food taste characteristics are desirable and implement those findings to their product. For example, if there was a change in the level of potato chips crunch that satisfies most of the consumers, the company will get their scientists to test and improve that chips while combing it into a certain product that will later be on the market as a new sensation.

The second factor that makes us eat junk food even though we know it is not good for our health is the combination of nutrients that has. The number of fats, proteins, and carbohydrates in junk food are combined to keep people coming back. The point is that our brain likes variety in every aspect, and food is no exception. So when you eat food that tastes the same all the time, there is no more pleasure in eating it, but junk food is made to give you response all the time. It is interesting to your brain and you keep eating it even though you sometimes are not even hungry because there are no sensors that can tell you to stop. That is one of the reasons why you can eat two bags of potato chips, and at times even start a third bag without even having second thoughts. Junk food in combination with binge eating problems can seriously affect a person's weight and health, which is why one of the important steps to deal with BED is to replace junk food with healthier options.

The biggest issue with junk food is that it will make you believe that you get everything you need from food (like nutrition), still, you will never feel really full. There will always be a place for more, and your body still won't receive everything it needs to perform all its basic actions. Junk food provides the number of calories that will send your brain a signal that it will provide energy, but your stomach won't have the feeling that it is full. This paradox is why overeating is not that rare and involves junk food in general.

One of the good things is that there is a way to reduce the craving for junk food. According to researchers, once you stop eating it often the craving will be reduced too. However, you must do it slowly; the answer is not shutting out junk food immediately. Start eating healthier, and at one point, you will remove junk food from your menu permanently. If you want to learn more about this transition period, you can also look under ''gene reprogramming'' since that is another way to call it. In both cases, the goal is the same, when you start changing your eating habits and eat healthy food instead, food junk will find its way out of your menu gradually. You will feel better about yourself, and your body will be happier too. There are a few things that might help you additionally in this process:

You should try to avoid eating convenience and packaged food for starters. If you don't have that kind of food in your house you won't eat it, it is that simple. Of course, this doesn't mean that your brain will stop wanting junk food because of that, but when it becomes a habit, it will be normal not to have processed food around at all.

The useful strategy for reducing junk food in terms of packaged and processed food is known as ''outer ring''. The key feature of this strategy is limiting yourself to buying only things that are on the ''outer rings'' of the market, such as meat, fruits, eggs, veggies, and so on. The mindset you should have is that things on the "outer ring" are healthy while those who are in the ring are not. There is also a rule that you can follow to avoid buying junk food. It is called a five-ingredient rule and it is based on the premise that if a product has more than 5 ingredients in it, you shouldn't buy it. This way you will choose more natural options when you enter the store.

There are other ways to find various food sensations that can make you enjoy your meal without turning to junk food all the time. Experimenting with food can be fun, and nowadays with the internet, the possibilities are countless. There is a large number of recipes that you can find and make tasty food that is both healthy and tasty. So, we can conclude that stereotypes about healthy food being bland aren't really true. And although junk food can be really tempting, there is a way to gradually replace it, or at least to find the healthiest versions of it. You can produce various food sensations by mixing food, using similar principles of junk food but with healthy ingredients. Still, the main reason for overeating and junk food is usually stress.

As we explained, when we feel stressed, our bodies release hormones, and our brains release chemicals that trigger our cravings. And since junk food is the fastest and "tastiest" way to satisfy these stress cravings, we end up binge eating over and over again. It can pull you back to junk food if the addiction is still strong or if your body is stronger than your will-power overpowered by bad emotions. So, the alternative is not only eating healthier but finding different ways to deal with stress. When binge eating we are actually trying to deal and to get rid of our emotions, but if we find another way than it will be easier to resist junk food too. In the beginning, mediation or some simple physical exercises might be just what you need to begin your change towards the healthier version of self.

An Extra Benefit of Cooking At Home

It is said that in the USA more and more families don't have the opportunity to enjoy a homemade meal due to the lack of time or just the possibility of buying cheap convenience food. First of all, homemade meals are not just about food. It is a process of socialization, an activity where everyone feels better, and ultimately, eats healthier. It provides a deeper connection between people.

There are many benefits that you can have from cooking. And these benefits are important for children and adults equally. For starters, you will feel happier, it was proven in multiple studies that people who enjoy home-made meals don't crave that much fat and sugar, and they eat healthier food in general. More importantly, this kind of connection is good for mental health. Dealing with stress, anxiety and depression are all issues that can be helped with a little bit of happiness. Some even claim that if a person eats more than five homemade meals weekly it will prolong its life.

Now, to get back to mental health benefits which are even greater when you prepare food with other people. At times, these group meals influence our mood even when we are not eating. The main reason for that is the fact that food and food preparation, in general, reinforce social connections. It is a way of showing yourself that you belong and it can help reduce depression. Eventually, preparing a meal with your family can even be interesting from a historical point of view since there are simple recipes passed from generation to generation in many houses.

If you are someone who cares about the planet and its environment, there is another benefit of homemade meals. They are not only saving your money because they are cheaper, but they are also saving the planet by reducing carbon footprint. The main advantage of cooking at home is that we can choose ingredients. So you can use vegetables or meat that is fresh, without relying on convenience foods. And it is even better if you have the opportunity to buy ingredients from local farmers. You can even try growing a few spices on your balcony.

Many people say how they don't have enough time to prepare meals at home. Still, it is relatively easy to evaluate the real amount of your free time. Just write down your activities for one week. And when you calculate how much time is spent on social media or on your phone, you will realize that you can manage some time to prepare meals at least once a week. You can even cook food in advance and keep it in the freezer. It is still nutritious and healthy.

Healthy Fast Food Defined

By definition, fast food is a food that can come from many places, but first of all it is a food that is served quickly, and more importantly, prepared quickly. You can usually find it in take-out, sit-down, and delivery restaurants. The reason why fast food became so popular over the years is that it is cheap, usually has a good taste, and it is convenient for those who don't have time to prepare meals at home. Still, the main reason why fast food usually isn't healthy is that it is made from ingredients that are often the cheapest (the cheapest meat that usually has a high level of fats, they add sugar in it and they add a lot of sodium).

Since many people started talking about health issues that can be caused by junk food (and fast food in most of the cases is considered to be a type of junk food), many fast-food restaurants have started offering healthier options. Before it wasn't really possible to have a few fast-food menu items with vegetables or fruits, but now there are more and more items that can be eaten as a meal without a sense of guilt. It is said that if an item offered in fast food has less than 500 calories, it can be considered healthy. Still fewer calories don't mean healthier meals. But it is better to have that option if it is really necessary to eat out.

So, we can define healthy fast food as more preferable fast food. Still, you shouldn't eat this ''version' of fast food all the time, you can make or order some healthy fast food meal for a change, but not as something that you eat regularly.

Easy To Cook, Fast to Prepare, and It Tastes Yummy

Since we mentioned that it is good to prepare some healthy fast food meal for a change, here are some options that are fast and easy.

If you like chicken, then chicken nuggets will be a great way to eat something great while making it in no time. Again, for calorie-trackers, chicken nuggets have approximately 258 calories. You can make a crust for them with almond for example. Chicken nuggets are great for binge eaters because they will make you feel full which means that you won't be tempted to overeat, and since you are preparing them at home, frying them in olive oil can reduce even more calories.

Another healthier fast food option can be cheeseburger sliders. They have approximately 267 calories and they are actually an epitome when it comes to fast food. Still, there is a huge difference in making these sliders at home and ordering them from the local fast food. Just make sure that you buy grass-fed beef because it has fewer calories.

A meal that has more calories than the previous two, but can be a great treat is chicken and bacon melt with ranch and cheddar. The number of calories if around 469, but since it is not a thing that you will prepare every day, you should enjoy it a bit. In comparison, this meal in every fast food has more than 600 calories. Imagine eating it whenever you have a binge episode? That is why it is way better to make a homemade version and if there are some ingredients that you don't like, you can just leave them out.

One of the most popular foods in every fast food in the whole world is French fries. Of course, there is an option of making them at home, and with 200 calories per portion, it should be a treat that makes you and all your friends happy. Buying domestic potato is the best option since it has the highest amounts of vitamin C. Still, you should avoid eating French fries with things like ketchup. Use some organic dips instead.

Egg Mc Muffins are also easy to make and fast too. Several calories are just a little bit above the French fries (237), and as you know already, eggs are a great source of protein. Fun fact is that when you order an egg Mc Muffin in fast food you will get a meal with over 400 calories and full of sodium. So instead of doing that, just take 10-15 minutes of your free time and make it for yourself.

Organic, Local, or Seasonal Ingredients

Consuming seasonal, local, and organic foods are one of the simplest ways to reconnect with nature and eat the best from it. This kind of food provides your body everything it needs to become healthy and to increase your mental health and feeling of satisfaction. Instead of buying products that are tasteless and don't have the right amount of nutrition, you can start with small changes and buying some basic ingredients first and then spread that circle. For example, seasonal vegetables and fruits are cheaper, thus it is easier for your budget to keep preparing healthy meals. Also, seasonal food is fresh which means that you have more than one benefit. If veggies and fruits that you buy are from the local farmers, it means that they haven't traveled and that the product wasn't at any kind of risk. For example, if a fruit travels from a distant place and stays in storage for a long time, it will lose all its nutritional richness and it won't be of use to you. The same principle applies to meat products and fish. If you buy meat from someone that produces it locally, you are sure that it is fresh and that it wasn't indifferent transportation vehicles, different storages, touched by many hands, and so on and so on. Also, you make sure that there are no chemicals that stores often put into meat to make it look fresh even though it is not.

If you have a farmers market around, you should check it out. If you don't have any local farmers just ask in your store if some products came from somewhere close. Local, seasonal and organic foods are the best choice for your health, and in the long run for your wallet too.

Continuing On the Path of Mindful Eating and Living

Since most of us are trying to keep up with fast-paced lifestyles, it can be difficult to balance our real needs and the life we are leading. When you are constantly on the move, you are not able to listen to signals that your body sends you. That is why it is important to practice mindfulness. When you start applying mindfulness to your eating habits, you can learn how to recognize and deal with unhealthy behaviors and how to provide your body the attention it needs.

Your Personal Plan of Action

First of all, you need to learn how to slow down so your body can catch up with your brain. We have already mentioned this, so you know that you need at least 20 minutes to realize if you are full, otherwise you will overeat.

To make your personal plan on how to practice mindfulness you need to learn to recognize the signals your body sends to you.

Another important part of a personal plan of action is to start changing your eating environment. You can use many devices that were given in the previous sections, from snacks to fully prepared home-meals. You just need to make an eating plan in advance, that way you won't end up wandering or overeating at some fast-food restaurant.

You need to learn what motivates you and try to work with that motivation. The goal is to find the balance.

Ultimately, you should try to connect with food, think about it, and stop multitasking while eating. That way you will prevent yourself from eating without even realizing it.

Mindfulness Meditation Practice

Mindfulness meditation practices are quite straightforward and in practice very simple. You just need some comfortable place to sit, you need to focus on your breathing and keep returning your focus at the moment you realize that it is gone. There are simple steps that you should follow:

Take a seat wherever you can as long as it is comfortable.

Pay attention to your legs, your feet should be touching the floor.

Also, your upper body should be parallel with your arms.

Your chin should be dropped out a bit and then you have to focus on gazing downward.

After you get into position, you have to relax, keep focusing on your breath and sensations in your body. It is useful to practice by taking breaks before taking any physical action (for example if you are feeling itchy, take a pause rather than scratch).

After a minute, or whenever you are ready to lift your head and focus on body sensation. Take a short break and make a decision on how you want to spend the rest of the day.

In the beginning, this can last shortly, but in time, it can last as long as you need it. It is simple, but it doesn't mean that it easy. Anyhow, if you keep practicing, the results will follow.

Conclusion

Body size is actually never a problem. The bigger problem is the fact that eating disorders are reduced to stereotypes like some bodies are better than other bodies. Binge eating should never be seen as just a characteristic of fat people, or being too skinny doesn't mean that everyone would want to have anorexia. Dieting and its yo-yo effect can be observed as a part of the eating disorder hierarchy too. If we don't know how to recognize the food that we need we can end up having more problems than solutions. And it will be even more difficult to focus on other aspects of life. The restriction was never a solution, and it is definitely the root of a problem. Still, if you learn to listen to your body you will find a way to help yourself more.

www.ingramcontent.com/pod-product-compliance
Lightning Source LLC
Chambersburg PA
CBHW070954080526
44587CB00015B/2297